Student Workbook and Study Guide

Basic Statistics for the Behavioral Sciences

SIXTH EDITION

Gary W. Heiman
Buffalo State College

Prepared by

D. J. Hendricks
West Virginia University

Richard T. Walls
West Virginia University

WADSWORTH
CENGAGE Learning

Australia • Brazil • Japan • Korea • Mexico • Singapore • Spain • United Kingdom • United States

For product information and technology assistance, contact us at **Cengage Learning Customer & Sales Support, 1-800-354-9706**

For permission to use material from this text or product, submit all requests online at **www.cengage.com/permissions**
Further permissions questions can be emailed to **permissionrequest@cengage.com**

ISBN-13: 978-0-495-90959-0
ISBN-10: 0-495-90959-9

Wadsworth
20 Davis Drive
Belmont, CA 94002-3098
USA

Cengage Learning is a leading provider of customized learning solutions with office locations around the globe, including Singapore, the United Kingdom, Australia, Mexico, Brazil, and Japan. Locate your local office at: **www.cengage.com/global**

Cengage Learning products are represented in Canada by Nelson Education, Ltd.

To learn more about Wadsworth, visit **www.cengage.com/wadsworth**

Purchase any of our products at your local college store or at our preferred online store **www.CengageBrain.com**

Printed in the United States of America
1 2 3 4 5 6 7 14 13 12 11 10

Contents

Preface

This book is called a workbook and study guide, but it is actually a companion designed to travel with you down the road as you learn statistics. To become proficient in statistical procedures, you need to practice applying them. This workbook provides you with an opportunity to do this.

Each chapter corresponds to a chapter in the textbook. In addition, there is a review chapter called "Getting Ready for the Final Exam."

You should use the workbook *only* after you have completed the corresponding chapter in the textbook. First, seriously study the entire textbook chapter. Then review the chapter summary and determine whether you understand it. If you don't, return to the corresponding chapter section and review it again. Then work through the problems at the end of the chapter. When you think you're in good shape, use the workbook to practice identifying concepts, selecting procedures, and computing and interpreting answers. The questions are accompanied by the correct answer so you can check yourself as you go along. However, don't look at the answer until you are sure you either have the correct answer or have done everything possible to figure it out.

Each chapter begins with a list of what you need to know, with two sections: **You Should Learn** and **You Should Learn When, Why, and How to Use These Formulas.**

The next section, **One More Time** is a review of the important points covered in the chapter. It contains fill-in-the-blank items requiring one or a few words. Answers appear in the margin directly opposite each blank. Cover the answers while you fill in the blanks, but don't complete the whole section before checking your answers. Instead, as you finish each sentence, see if you have the correct answer. If you do not, think about why the answer given is correct. If you're lost at any point, return to the textbook and review the material.

Following "One More Time" is a self-test called **Now Do you Know?** It consists of a list of the symbols and key terms in the chapter. There are no answers provided here. If you cannot define a symbol or term on your own, return to "One More Time" or refer to your textbook.

The next section is called **Using What You Know.** It contains problems and questions in which you apply statistics to various situations. Answers to these problems are provided at the end of the workbook chapter. For many problems, answers to intermediate steps are provided, so if your final answer is different from the answer given, be sure to figure out why.

By now you should be ready for **The Test,** which contains questions that are good examples of potential multiple-choice test items. The answers to "The Test" also are provided at the end of the workbook chapter.

Good Luck!

Chapter 1
Introduction to Statistics

YOU SHOULD LEARN

1. The reason researchers use statistics.

2. The symbols used to represent scores and mathematical operations.

3. The order in which mathematical operations in a formula are performed.

4. The rules of rounding.

5. How to transform scores to a proportion and vice versa.

6. How to transform a proportion to a percent and vice versa.

7. How to create and read graphs.

ONE MORE TIME: A Review

Behavioral scientists use _____ as tools in their research. The scores   statistics

we measure in any type of research are called the _____. The most   data

important things for you to learn about statistics are _____ to use a   when

particular procedure, how to _____ the answer, and _____ the   compute; what

answer tells you. Statistics are used to _____ and _____ the   organize; summarize

data. Statistics also are used to _____ the results and to _____   communicate;
                                                                                                    conclude
what the data indicate. Remember, the only way to lean statistics is to

_____ statistics.   do

The symbols that stand for each score in a study are _____ and X

_____. $X - Y$ means X _____ Y. XY, $(X)Y$, $X(Y)$, and $(X)(Y)$ all Y; minus

mean X _____ Y. The symbol X^2 means we are to _____ X.   times; square

X; X

square root;
calculator

numerator

denominator

quantity; quantity

parentheses

multiplication;
division; addition
subtraction

two

three

up

down

transformation

comparable

proportion

divided

In other words, find _____ times _____. $\sqrt{X}$ means find the

_____ _____ of X. You'll probably want to use a _____

for this operation. In a fraction, the quantity above the dividing line is called

the _____ and the quantity below the dividing line is called the

_____.

    In statistical notation, parentheses, the square root sign, and the dividing

line in a fraction all imply the _____. We compute the _____

first, and then perform any other operations. Unless otherwise indicated, the

order in which we perform mathematical operations is first to compute

inside any _____, then to square or take a square root, then to perform

_____ or _____, and, finally, to perform _____ or

_____.

    When performing statistical calculations, we round off the final answer

to _____ decimal places *more* than are in the original scores. During

intermediate steps in calculation, we maintain at least _____

additional decimal places than are in the original scores. According to the

rounding rule, if the number is five or greater, round _____; if the

number is less than five, round _____.

    A systematic mathematical procedure for converting a set of scores to a

different set of scores is called a(n) _____. We transform scores to

make them easier to work with or to make different types of scores

_____. When we transform a score to a decimal number

between 0 and 1.0 that indicates a portion of the total, we have computed

a(n) _____. To transform a score to a proportion, the score is

_____ by the total. Conversely, to determine the score that constitutes a certain proportion, the proportion is _____ by the total. When we | multiplied

transform a score by computing a proportion and then multiplying the

proportion by 100, we have computed a(n) _____. | percent

When a graph is created, the length of the Y axis should be about

_____% to _____% of the length of the X axis. On any graph, | 60; 75

the scores on the X axis become larger positive as we read to the

_____, and the scores on the Y axis become larger positive as we read | right

_____. The X or Y axis is compressed using the symbol "//" whenever | upward

there is a substantial gap between _____ and the lowest X or Y score | zero (0)

being plotted.

When plotting a pair of X and Y scores, the "dot" on a graph is called

a(n) _____ _____. To read the values at a data point, we travel | data point

vertically from the X score to the data point; then we travel _____ to | horizontally

read the value of _____. So that a graph accurately reflects the pattern | Y

shown in the data, we must be careful in choosing the numbers we use to

_____ the X and Y axes. | label

NOW DO YOU KNOW?

statistics	order of mathematical operations
statistical notation	transformation
data	proportion
X	percent
Y	X axis
numerator	Y axis
denominator	data point

USING WHAT YOU KNOW

1. What are the goals of the statistics student?

2. For what purposes do researchers use statistics?

3. Unless otherwise indicated, what is the order in which mathematical operations are performed?

4. What are the rules for rounding?

5. To how many decimal places does one round off a final answer?

6. How is a proportion computed?

7. What is a percentage?

8. Round the following to two decimal places.

    a. 43.4555
    b. 0.9099
    c. 20.4
    d. 1.549
    e. 0.0004

9. For $X = 6.3$ and $Y = 2.1$, find M where

$$M = \frac{X^2 + Y}{Y^2}$$

10. For $X = 11.4$ and $Y = 4.8$, find J where

$$J = \frac{10 - \dfrac{\sqrt{Y^2 + X^2}}{Y^2}}{X}$$

11. For $X = 8$ and $Y = 0.3$, find M where

$$M = \left[\frac{(X + Y)^2}{Y}\right]\left[\frac{Y}{\sqrt{XY}}\right]$$

12. For $X = 13$ and $Y = 22$, find L where

$$L = \frac{X + Y - \dfrac{Y^2 + X^2}{\sqrt{Y + X}}}{\sqrt{Y^2 - X^2}}$$

13. In a statistics class 60% of the 75 students passed.

   a. What proportion of the class passed?
   b. How many students passed?

14. A student answers 12 of 60 test questions correctly.

   a. What is the *proportion* of questions answered correctly?
   b. What is the *percent* of questions answered correctly?

15. On an exam with 50 questions, 60% correct is a D, 70% is a C, 80% is a B, and 90% is an A.

   a. If a student has 35 correct answers, what is the student's grade?
   b. How many correct answers must a student have in order to pass (a grade of D)?
   c. How many wrong answers can a student have and still receive an A?

16. Following are data from three studies. Graph the data from each.

Study A			Study B			Study C	
X	Y		X	Y		X	Y
1	5		1	10		1	3
2	5		2	9		2	5
3	5		3	8		3	7
4	5		4	7		4	9
5	5		5	6		5	11
6	5		6	5		6	13

17. A beginning statistics student has conducted a study on the effectiveness of a new diet and found the diet to be extremely effective. He prepared the following graph to show the typical weight loss after each week of his study:

Weight Loss

Week 1   10 lbs
Week 2   14 lbs
Week 3   21 lbs
Week 4   25 lbs
Week 5   29 lbs
Week 6   30 lbs

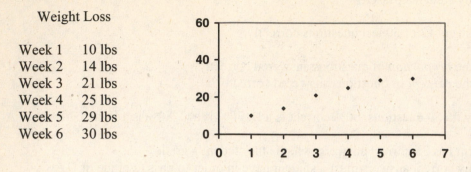

a. Why does it appear that the diet was a flop?
b. Create your own graph so that the data more accurately demonstrate the effectiveness of the diet.

THE TEST

1. The most important thing you will learn from the textbook is

   a. How to compute the correct answer using statistical formulas.
   b. When and why to use procedures and how to interpret the answers.
   c. How to derive a useful statistical formula from one that is less useful.
   d. How to efficiently use a calculator to compute answers to statistical formulas.

2. For $X = 9$ and $Y = 8$, what is the correct answer for $P = \dfrac{X}{Y}$ using the rules of rounding?

   a. 1.1250
   b. 1.125
   c. 1.12
   d. 1.13

3. A systematic mathematical procedure for converting one set of scores into a different set of scores is called a

   a. transformation.
   b. statistic.
   c. theoretical manipulation.
   d. graph.

4. When there is a set of parentheses in an equation, what would you normally do first?

   a. Perform operations outside the parentheses.
   b. Perform operations within the parentheses.
   c. Multiply by a constant to remove the parentheses.
   d. Divide by a constant to remove the parentheses.

5. Unless otherwise indicated, which of the following is the correct order to follow in carrying out mathematical operations in a formula after performing operations within a set of parentheses?

   a. Add or subtract, then multiply or divide, then square or take the square root.
   b. Multiply or divide, then square or take the square root, then add or subtract.
   c. Square or take the square root, then add or subtract, then multiply or divide.
   d. Square or take the square root, then multiply or divide, then add or subtract.

ANSWERS TO USING WHAT YOU KNOW

1. The goals are to learn when and why to use each procedure and how to interpret the answer.

2. They use statistics to organize and summarize scores, to communicate the results of the data, and to draw conclusions about what the data indicate.

3. Square a quantity or find its square root first, then perform multiplication or division and, finally, perform addition or subtraction.

4. When rounding, if the number is five or greater than five, round up. If the number is less than five, round down.

5. One rounds off a final answer to two more decimal places than are in the original scores.

6. A proportion equals the score divided by the total.

7. A percent is a proportion multiplied by 100.

8. a. 43.46
   b. 0.91
   c. 20.40
   d. 1.55
   e. 0.00

9. $M = \dfrac{6.3^2 + 2.1}{2.1^2} = \dfrac{39.69 + 2.1}{4.41} = \dfrac{41.79}{4.41} = 9.476$

10. $J = \dfrac{10 - \dfrac{\sqrt{23.04 + 129.96}}{23.04}}{11.4} = \dfrac{10 - \dfrac{12.3693}{23.04}}{11.4} = \dfrac{10 - 0.5369}{11.4} = \dfrac{9.4631}{11.4} = 0.830$

11. $M = \left[\dfrac{(8 + 0.3)^2}{0.3}\right]\left[\dfrac{0.3}{\sqrt{(8)(0.3)}}\right] = \left[\dfrac{68.890}{0.3}\right]\left[\dfrac{0.3}{1.549}\right] = [229.633][0.194] = 44.55$

12. $L = \dfrac{13 + 22 - \dfrac{22^2 + 13^2}{\sqrt{22^2 + 13^2}}}{\sqrt{22^2 - 13^2}} = \dfrac{13 + 22 - \dfrac{484 + 169}{\sqrt{35}}}{\sqrt{484 - 169}} = \dfrac{13 + 22 - \dfrac{653}{5.916}}{17.748}$

$= \dfrac{35 - 110.379}{17.748} = -4.25$

13. a. 0.60
    b. 45

14. a. 0.20
    b. 20%

15. a. c
    b. 30
    c. 5

16.

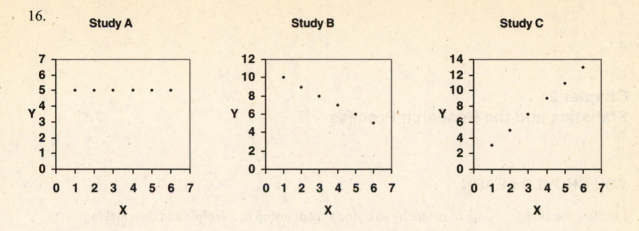

17. Because each label on the *Y* axis spans 20 pounds, the graph gives the impression that relatively little weight was lost.

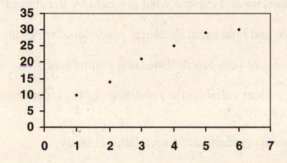

ANSWERS TO THE TEST

1. b   2. d   3. a   4. b   5. d

Chapter 2
Statistics and the Research Process

YOU SHOULD LEARN

1. How we study the laws of nature by studying a relationship in a sample and then making inferences about the relationship in the population.

2. How whether a sample is representative or unrepresentative affects inferences about the population.

3. How to recognize a relationship and explain what is meant by the strength of a relationship.

4. When and why descriptive and inferential statistical procedures are used.

5. The similarities and differences between statistics and parameters.

6. How to identify the independent variable, the conditions of the independent variable, and the dependent variable in an experiment.

7. The difference between an experiment and a correlational study.

8. The different characteristics of scores.

9. The four different types of measurement scales and the difference between continuous and discrete scales.

ONE MORE TIME: A Review

	The complete group of individuals to which a law of nature applies is called
population	the _____. The subset of those individuals we actually measure and
sample	that is intended to represent the larger group is called the _____. The
participants	individuals we measure in a sample are called the _____. In research,
sample	we measure the individuals in the _____ and then use those scores to
infer	estimate or _____ the scores we would expect in the population. In
	order for our inferences about a population to be accurate, the sample must

be _____ of the population. A representative sample accurately | representative

reflects the _____ of the population. However, a sample may not | behaviors

accurately reflect the behaviors of the population, in which case the sample

is _____ of the population. After the population and sample have | unrepresentative

been identified for a study, we define the situation and behaviors we want to

observe and measure. To do this, we select our _____. | variables

Variables and Relationships

Anything that, when measured produces different scores is called a(n)

_____. A variable that reflects different amounts or quantities is | variable

called a(n) _____ variable. A variable that reflects different qualities | quantitative

or categories is called a(n) _____ variable. In research, we seek to | qualitative

study the _____ between our variables. | relationship

When the scores on one variable tend to change in a consistent manner

as the corresponding scores on another variable change, a(n) _____ | relationship

exists. When we talk about relationships in statistics, we use the term

_____. How consistently the scores on one variable are associated | association

with the corresponding scores on the other variable is referred to as the

_____ of the relationship. When a group of similar Y scores are | strength

associated with one _____ score and a different group of similar | X

_____ scores are associated with the next X score, there is a(n) | Y

_____ relationship. | strong

One of the reasons that scores are not perfectly associated is because

no two people are exactly the same. This is called _____ _____ | individual differences

among participants. If, as the scores on one variable change, there is no

consistent pattern of change on the other variable, then there is _____ | no

relationship	_____ . We describe a relationship using the phrase "changes in the Y
function of; X	variable as (a) _____ _____ changes in the _____
	variable."

Descriptive and Inferential Statistics

The statistical procedures allowing us to organize and summarize the

descriptive	characteristics of a sample of scores are called _____ statistics.

Although descriptive statistics give us a general understanding of the data,

every	they do not precisely describe _____ sample score. Another use for
predict	descriptive statistics is they allow us to _____ when a behavior will
relationship	occur by using the _____ between two variables.

The statistical procedures allowing us to draw conclusions about the

inferential	population using the scores from a sample are called _____

procedures. We know we usually cannot measure every individual in a

population. Therefore, we must use the scores in a sample to make

inferences	_____ about the population.

A number describing a characteristic of a population is called a(n)

parameter	_____ . A number describing characteristics of a sample is called a(n)
statistic	_____ . The symbols used for different statistics are letters from the
English	_____ alphabet. The symbols used for different parameters are letters
Greek; statistics	from the _____ alphabet. Descriptive procedures yield _____ ,
parameters	while inferential procedures estimate _____ . How a study is laid out is
design	called its _____ . One of the challenges in statistics is knowing which
statistical procedures	_____ _____ should be used with different designs.

Experiments and Correlational Studies

When a researcher attempts to demonstrate a relationship by controlling or manipulating a variable, he or she is conducting a(n) _____. When the researcher attempts to demonstrate a relationship by simply measuring scores on two variables, he or she is performing a(n) _____ _____.

experiment

correlational study

In an experiment, the variable that is manipulated by the experimenter is called the _____ variable. The specific situation created by each amount or category of the independent variable is called a(n) _____. The variable used to measure participants' scores is called the _____ variable. When an experiment demonstrates a relationship, there are _____ scores on the dependent variable associated with each condition of the independent variable. Descriptive statistics are used only on the scores from the _____ variable.

independent

condition

dependent

different

dependent

The Characteristics of Scores

The particular descriptive or inferential procedure that we use is partly determined by the measurement _____ of the variable. When a score is used to identify a quality or category (rather than an amount), we have a(n) _____ scale. When a score cannot be zero and indicates a rank order, we have a(n) _____ scale. When the scores measure an actual amount, but there is no true zero, we have a(n) _____ scale. When the scores measure an actual amount and zero indicates a truly zero amount, we have a(n) _____ scale. There is an equal unit of measurement between adjacent scores only with _____ and _____ scales.

scale

nominal

ordinal

interval

ratio

interval; ratio

continuous	When we measure a variable in which decimals make sense, we have a(n) _____ variable. When decimals do not make sense, we have a(n)
discrete	_____ variable. The special case of a discrete variable in which there are
dichotomous	only two amounts or categories of the variable is called a(n) _____ variable.

NOW DO YOU KNOW?

population	parameter
sample	design
participants	experiment
representative	independent variable
random sample	condition (level, treatment)
variable	dependent variable
relationship	correlational study
strength of a relationship	nominal scale
individual differences	ordinal scale
as a function of	interval scale
data points	ratio scale
descriptive statistics	continuous scale
inferential statistics	discrete scale
statistic	dichotomous

USING WHAT YOU KNOW

1. What is the difference between a population and a sample?

2. What are the differences between statistics and parameters in their use and symbols?

3. What is a representative sample?

4. What is a random sample?

5. What is a variable?

6, Give two reasons why a relationship may not be perfectly consistent.

7. Compare and contrast descriptive and inferential statistics.

8. Describe and contrast experiments and correlational studies.

9. Define the four major types of measurement scales.

10. Of the three sets of data that follow, which sample shows the strongest relationship?

Sample A		Sample B		Sample C	
X	*Y*	*X*	*Y*	*X*	*Y*
1	5	1	5	1	5
1	5	1	6	1	6
1	5	2	7	2	5
2	7	2	8	2	6
2	7	2	9	3	6
3	9	3	10	3	5
3	9	3	11	4	6

11. For the data sets presented in problem 10, which sample shows the weakest relationship?

12. Following are graphs of data from three studies. Does each graph indicate a relationship? How do you know?

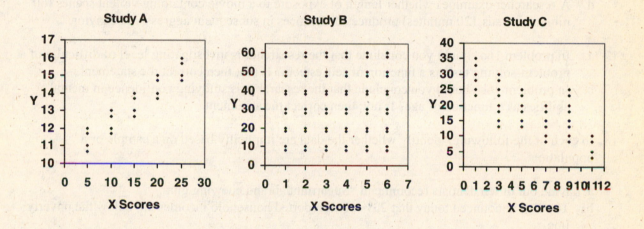

13. Which study in problem 12 demonstrated the greatest degree of association between the variables? Why?

14. For each of the following research projects, indicate whether a researcher would be most likely to study the relationship by conducting an experiment or a correlational study:

a. A comparison of the effects of different amounts of caffeine consumed in one hour on speed of completing a complex motor task.
b. An investigation of the relationship between number of extracurricular activities and GPA.
c. An examination of the relationship between the number of pairs of sneakers a person owns and the person's athletic success.
d. A comparison of the effects of three types of perfume on perceived sexual attractiveness.
e. An investigation of the relationship between GPA and the ability to pay off school loans.
f. A comparison of the effects of different amounts of beer consumed on a person's mood.

15. A researcher conducted an experiment.

    a.   If she wants to test whether there is a relationship between her independent and dependent variables, what type of statistical procedures should she use?

    b.   What does it mean if she finds the scores of her dependent variable change consistently with the different levels of her independent variable?

    c.   If she finds a relationship, what will she want to do?

16. In each of the following experiments, identify the independent variable, the conditions of the independent variable, and the dependent variable:

    a.   A researcher studies whether participants' self-esteem is influenced by whether they have completed an easy or a difficult problem-solving task.

    b.   A researcher compares young, middle-aged, and senior citizen adults with respect to how much confidence they have in their mental abilities.

    c.   A researcher investigates whether people estimate the duration of a time period differently as a function of whether they view three, five, or seven pictures per minute during the period.

    d.   A researcher examines whether length of exposure to a movie containing violent scenes (60 minutes versus 120 minutes) produces differences in subsequent aggressive behavior.

17. a.   In problem 16a should you conclude that the researcher is investigating level of difficulty of a problem-solving task as a function of self-esteem? If not, then correct the statement.

    b.   In problem 16b should you conclude that the researcher is studying confidence in mental abilities as a function of age? If not, then correct the statement.

18. In each of the following, identify whether the data are implicitly based on a sample or a population:

    a.   Nine out of ten dentists recommend "Sugarmint" brand chewing gum.

    b.   The IRS announced today that 23% of all reported household incomes are below the poverty line.

    c.   The average height of professional basketball players in the NBA is six feet, nine inches.

    d.   Based on a survey of major cities, the national crime rate increases during the summer months.

19. For each of the following statements, determine what is the sample and what is the population. Also, determine whether the sample would be considered representative.

    a.   200 freshmen at State College were selected randomly and asked to indicate their opinions as to how prepared they felt to attend this school.

    b.   All 40 teachers at North High School were asked to complete a survey on methods of instruction used in the state's schools.

    c.   A psychology student was asked to report on the difficulty of questions asked in the recent state licensing exam.

    d.   In a national survey of counselors 2,000 randomly selected counselors were asked to rate their job-related anxiety level.

20. In the following chart, complete the row opposite each variable:

Variable	Continuous, Discrete, or Dichotomous	Type of Measurement Scale
nationality	_____	_____
hand pressure	_____	_____
baseball team rank	_____	_____
letter grade on a test	_____	_____
pregnancy	_____	_____
checkbook balance	_____	_____

THE TEST

1. A number describing a characteristic of a sample of scores is a

    a. parameter.
    b. nominal scale.
    c. variable.
    d. statistic.

2. Gender is an example of a(n)

    a. ratio scale.
    b. nominal scale.
    c. ordinal scale.
    d. interval scale.

3. Statistical procedures used to make decisions about a population based on the scores from a sample are called

    a. descriptive statistics.
    b. correlational statistics.
    c. inferential statistics.
    d. no statistical procedures can prove that one variable causes another variable to change.

4. Which of the following is true regarding random sampling?

    a. When used, it guarantees that the sample will be representative.
    b. It is not necessary when nominal variables are used.
    c. It is possible to randomly obtain a sample that is not representative.
    d. It is necessary in correlational but not in experimental research.

5. If we decide to compare the recall of word lists by 40-year-olds, 50-year-olds, and 60-year-olds, the age variable would be best described as

    a. a quasi-independent variable.
    b. a true independent variable.
    c. the dependent variable.
    d. a dichotomous variable.

ANSWERS TO USING WHAT YOU KNOW

1. A population is every individual to which a law of nature applies. A population usually is very large. A sample is a subset of individuals from the population. A sample usually is meant to represent the population.

2. Statistics describe the characteristics of a sample and are symbolized by English letters. Parameters describe the characteristics of a population and are symbolized by Greek letters.

3. A representative sample is a sample that accurately reflects the population.

4. A random sample is one in which individuals from the population are randomly selected to be in the sample.

5. A variable is anything that, when measured, produces different scores.

6. Two reasons why a relationship may not be perfectly consistent are extraneous influences and individual differences.

7. Descriptive statistics are used to organize, summarize, and describe the characteristics of a sample. Inferential statistics are used to decide whether the sample is representative of the population.

8. In an experiment the researcher has control over and manipulates one of the variables (the independent variable). In a correlational study the researcher simply measures the participant's scores on two variables.

9. A nominal scale identifies a quality or category. An ordinal scale involves scores that indicate rank order, units of measurement between scores are unequal, and there is no zero. An interval scale measures an amount, units between scores are equal, and negative numbers are allowed. A ratio scale measures an amount, units are equal, there is a true zero, and negative numbers are allowed.

10. Sample A.

11. Sample C.

12. A relationship is indicated in Study A and Study C. In each, as the scores on one variable change, the scores on the other variable change in a consistent fashion. This does not occur in Study B, and so no relationship is indicated.

13. Study A, because there is the smallest range of different Y scores at each X.

14. a. Experiment.
    b. Correlational study.
    c. Correlational study.
    d. Experiment.
    e Correlational study.
    f. Experiment.

15. a. She should use inferential procedures.
    b. It means she has found evidence of a relationship.
    c. She will want to draw inferences about the population with respect to her variables.

16. a. The independent variable is difficulty of the task; the conditions are easy and difficult; and the dependent variable is self-esteem.
    b. The independent variable is age; the conditions are young, middle-aged, and senior citizen; and the dependent variable is confidence in their mental abilities.
    c. The independent variable is number of pictures viewed per minute; the conditions are three, five, and seven pictures per minute; and the dependent variable is estimated duration of the time period.
    d. The independent variable is length of exposure to the movie; the conditions are 60 and 120 minutes; and the dependent variable is amount of aggressive behavior.

17. a. No; the researcher is investigating self-esteem as a function of level of difficulty of the problem-solving task.
    b. Yes, that is correct.

18. a. Sample.
    b. Population.
    c. Population.
    d. Sample.

19. a. Sample–200 freshmen; population–all freshmen at State College; probably representative because random selection and a large sample size were used.
    b. Sample–40 teachers; population–all teachers in the state; probably not representative because a random sample was not taken and teachers at one school would likely not be representative of all teachers in the state.
    c. Sample–one psychology student who has taken the state licensing exam; population–all students who took the exam; probably not representative because no random sampling was used and one student would likely not be representative of all those who took the exam.
    d. Sample–2,000 counselors; population–all counselors in the country; probably representative because random sampling was used and a large sample size was selected.

20.

Variable	Continuous, Discrete, or Dichotomous	Type of Measurement Scale
nationality	discrete	nominal
hand pressure	continuous	ratio
baseball team rank	discrete	ordinal
letter grade on a test	discrete	ordinal
pregnancy	dichotomous	nominal
checkbook balance	discrete	interval

ANSWERS TO THE TEST

1. d   2. b   3. c   4. c   5. a

Chapter 3
Frequency Distributions and Percentiles

YOU SHOULD LEARN

1. The meaning of simple frequency, relative frequency, and cumulative frequency.

2. The difference between a bar graph, a histogram, and a polygon and when to use each.

3. How to read and interpret a normal curve.

4. How to describe normal, skewed, bimodal, and rectangular distributions.

5. How to calculate relative frequencies and percentiles.

6. How to create tables and graphs showing simple, relative, and cumulative frequency.

7. How the proportion of the total area under the normal curve corresponds to the relative frequency of scores.

YOU SHOULD LEARN WHEN, WHY, AND HOW TO USE THESE FORMULAS

1. The formula for computing a score's relative frequency is

$$\text{Relative frequency} = \frac{f}{N}$$

2. The formula for computing a score's pecentile is

$$\text{Percentile} = \left(\frac{cf}{N}\right)(100)$$

ONE MORE TIME: A Review

The number of times a score occurs in a study is called its _____. We	frequency
indicate frequency using the lowercase letter _____. Any organized set	f
of data is called a(n) _____, so a distribution that organizes scores	distribution
based on their frequency is called a(n) _____ _____. The way to	frequency distribution

graph or

table

display a frequency distribution is by creating either a(n) _____ or a(n)

_____.

      More specifically, the number of times a score occurs in the data is the

simple frequency

score

highest; possible

lowest

frequency; score

number

score's _____ _____. To show simple frequency in a table, use

two columns. The left-hand column is labeled _____. At the top of this

column is the _____ score in the data. Below it are all _____

whole-number scores in order to the _____ score that occurred. The

right-hand column is the _____. For each _____ shown in the

left-hand column, the right-hand column indicates the _____ of times

it occurred in the data set. The total of all frequencies in a sample equals

N; number

_____, which is the total _____ of scores in the sample.

Graphing Simple Frequency Distributions

To graph a frequency distribution, the values of the scores are plotted along

X

Y

bar

nominal or ordinal

the _____ axis, and each score's frequency is plotted along the

_____ axis. A graph with adjacent bars that do not touch is called a(n)

_____ graph. A bar graph describes scores that are measured using

a(n) _____ or a(n) _____ scale of measurement. We should

always use a bar graph when the variable represented by the scores is

discrete; height

_____. In a bar graph, the _____ of each bar reflects that score's

frequency.

      When the adjacent bars of a graph touch, the graph is called a(n)

histogram; small

interval or ratio

_____. A histogram describes a(n) _____ number of scores that

are measured using either a(n) _____ or _____ scale. As with

bar graphs, the height of the bars in a histogram indicates that score's

_____. Even though the scores in a study appear discrete, if the | frequency

underlying variable is theoretically _____, you should use a histogram. | continuous

When a frequency graph is created by connecting adjacent data points

with straight lines, the graph is called a(n) _____. A polygon describes | polygon

a(n) _____ range of scores that are measured using a(n) _____ | large; interval

or _____ scale. To read the frequency of a score from a polygon, | ratio

locate the score on the _____ axis, move upward until you reach the | X

_____ of the polygon, and move _____ to locate the | line; horizontally

_____ of the score. | frequency

Types of Simple Frequency Distributions

The distribution that forms a symmetrical, bell-shaped curve is known as the

_____ distribution. On a normal curve, the score that occurs most | normal

frequently is the score in the _____ of the distribution, and the scores | middle

that occur relatively infrequently are the _____ scores. The portions of | extreme

the curve containing low-frequency, extreme scores are called the

_____ of the distribution. The ideal normal curve is based on a(n) | tails

_____ number of scores. Because of this, the tails of such a | infinite

distribution _____, but never touch, the _____ axis. The normal | approach; X

curve is important because it is a very _____ distribution in the | common

behavioral sciences.

When a distribution forms a nonsymmetrical polygon with only one

distinct tail, the distribution is call a(n) _____ distribution. When the | skewed

tail is at the extreme low scores, the distribution is _____ skewed; | negatively

when the tail is at the extreme high scores, the distribution is _____ | positively

skewed.

A symmetrical distribution with two areas in which there are scores of

bimodal relatively high frequency is called a(n) _____ distribution. A symmetrical

distribution in which the extreme scores have the same frequencies as the

rectangular middle scores is called a(n) _____ distribution.

Relative Frequency and the Normal Curve

When we compute the proportion of time a score occurs in a set of data, we are

relative frequency computing the score's _____ _____. The symbol for relative

rel.f frequency is _____. A score's relative frequency is computed by dividing

f; N the score's _____ by _____. The sum of all relative frequencies in a

1.0 sample equals _____.

When we compute the frequency of the scores that occurred at or below a

cumulative frequency particular score, we are computing that score's _____ _____. The

cf symbol for cumulative frequency is _____. A score's cumulative

frequency is the frequency of the score plus the frequencies of all the scores

below _____ it. The cumulative frequency of the highest score in the data must

N equal _____. When we compute the percentage of the scores that

occurred at or below a particular score, we are computing that score's

percentile _____. To compute a score's percentile, we must first know its

cf _____.

On the normal curve, if we draw a vertical line through the middle score,

0.50 then the proportion of scores to the left of the line is _____ and the

0.50 proportion of scores to the right of the line is _____. Because of this, a

proportion of the total area under the curve indicates the proportion of time the

relative frequency associated scores occurred, which is their _____ _____.

Computing Cumulative Frequency and Percentile

When we compute the frequency of all scores at or below a particular score,

this is called the _____ _____ for that score. To calculate the   cumulative frequency

percentile for a score, we _____ the cumulative frequency by N and   divide

then _____ that by 100.   multiply

Grouped Frequency Distributions

When a distribution examines each score individually, it is called a(n)

_____ distribution. When scores are combined into small groups, we   ungrouped

have a(n) _____ distribution.   grouped

NOW DO YOU KNOW?

f N rel. f cf

frequency
distribution
normal distribution
simple frequency
simple frequency distribution
bar graph
histogram
frequency polygon
normal curve
tails
negatively skewed distribution

positively skewed distribution
bimodal distribution
rectangular distribution
relative frequency
relative frequency distribution
total area under the normal curve
cumulative frequency
percentile
ungrouped distribution
grouped distribution

USING WHAT YOU KNOW

1. a.   What is a distribution?
    b.   What is a simple frequency distribution?

2. In graphing data, when is a bar graph created and when is a histogram or polygon created?

3. A scientist asked students to indicate whether a test was easy, somewhat difficult, or very difficult. She wants to graph the simple frequency distribution of these data. What type of graph should she create? Why?

4. What does it mean when a score is in one of the tails of the normal distribution?

5. Describe the shapes of normal, positively skewed, negatively skewed, bimodal, and rectangular distributions when graphed.

6. A professor observes that a distribution of test scores is negatively skewed. What does this tell the professor about the difficulty of the test? How do you know?

7. If you are told that your score on an intelligence test is at the 75th percentile, what does this tell you?

8. The scores on the final exam in a large introductory psychology class are known to be positively skewed.

   a. What would this indicate about the difficulty of the test?
   b. If your test score is in the tail of this distribution, what should you conclude about your performance?

9. What is the difference between

   a. a score's simple frequency and its relative frequency?
   b. a score's cumulative frequency and its percentile?

10. In a test on summarizing scores using frequency distributions and percentiles, you are given a small sample of raw scores. You are to determine the simple frequencies, relative frequencies, and cumulative frequencies and put them into a table.

    a. What should you put into the left-hand column of this complete table?
    b. When you add up all the simple frequencies, what should the total equal?
    c. When you add up all the relative frequencies, what should this total equal?
    d. What should the cumulative frequency for the highest score equal?

11. Explain why we can compute a score's percentile by finding the proportion of the area under the normal curve to the left of the score and multiplying it by 100.

12. The following normal distribution is based on a sample of data. The shaded area represents 13% of the area under the curve.

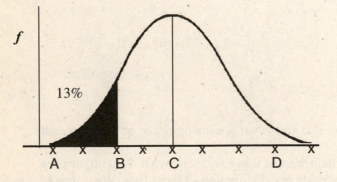

[Problem continues on the next page.]

a. What is the *rel. f* of scores between A and B?
b. What is the *rel. f* of scores between A and C?
c. What is the *rel. f* of scores between B and C?
d. Rank-order A, B, C, and D to reflect the order of scores from the highest to the lowest frequency.
e. Rank-order A, B, C, and D to reflect the order of scores from the highest to the lowest score.

13. A study was performed to determine the blood types of a group of astronauts. Create a simple frequency distribution for the data listed. Then, graph it. Order the blood types as B, AB−, A−, O, and A, with type B as the "highest score."

Subject	Blood Type	Subject	Blood Type
1	A	11	AB−
2	O	12	B
3	A−	13	A
4	O	14	A
5	B	15	O
6	A−	16	AB−
7	A	17	O
8	B	18	O
9	AB−	19	O
10	A	20	O

14. If you had to label the shape of the distribution in problem 13, what would you call it?

15. A group of students received the following grades on an exam:

87 83 83 81 84 86 83 86 85 85 86 84 87 86 87
87 86 85 85 86 86 87 85 83 81 87 86 86 86

Construct a table showing simple, relative, and cumulative frequency for these data. Then graph the cumulative frequency distribution.

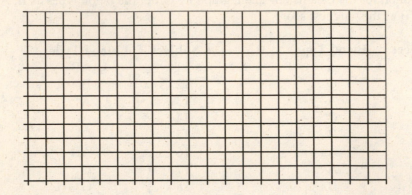

16. a. In a researcher's normal distribution, 35% of the area under the curve is to the right of the score of 70. At what percentile is 70?
     b. The middle score in the distribution is 60. What is the percentile of this score?
     c. What is the relative frequency of scores between 60 and 70?

17. A researcher obtained the following data:

Score	f	rel. f	cf
25	4		
24	5		
23	6		
22	6		
21	8		
20	7		
19	5		
18	4		
17	5		

     a. Compute the relative frequency and cumulative frequency of each score.
     b. How do you check that the relative frequencies are correct?
     c. How do you check that the cumulative frequencies are correct?

18. For the data in problem 17

     a. list the original set of raw scores from which this frequency distribution was generated.
     b. Is the distribution positively skewed, negatively skewed, or normal?

THE TEST

1. When would you graph a simple frequency using a polygon?

   a. When the variable is nominal and involves relatively few scores.
   b. When the variable is ordinal and involves many different scores.
   c. When the variable is interval or ratio and involves relatively few scores.
   d. When the variable is interval or ratio and involves many different scores.

2. If a distribution forms a symmetrical, bell shape in which extreme high and low scores occur relatively infrequently, it would be called a _____ distribution.

   a. negatively skewed
   b. positively skewed
   c. normal
   d. rectangular

3. The frequency of all scores at or below a given score is called the score's _____

   a. cumulative frequency.
   b. relative frequency.
   c. simple frequency.
   d. percentile.

4. The proportion of the total area under the normal curve at certain scores corresponds to the

   a. simple frequency of those scores.
   b. relative frequency of those scores.
   c. cumulative frequency of those scores.
   d. percentile of those scores.

5. We create a bar graph when

   a. there is only a small range of different scores.
   b. the scores are measured using a nominal or ordinal scale.
   c. there is a wide range of interval or ratio scores.
   d. the graph shows relative or cumulative frequency.

ANSWERS TO USING WHAT YOU KNOW

1. a. A distribution is an organized set of data.
   b. A simple frequency distribution shows the number of times each score occurs in a set of data.

2. A bar graph is created with nominal or ordinal data; a histogram or a polygon is created with interval or ratio data.

3. She should create a bar graph. "Easy," "somewhat difficult," and "very difficult" implies a rank order; thus, she has ordinal data, which require a bar graph.

4. When a score is in a tail of the normal distribution, it is an extreme score. It is relatively far away from the middle of the distribution and occurs with a relatively low frequency.

5. A normal distribution is bell-shaped and symmetrical. A positively skewed distribution is nonsymmetrical and has a distinct tail over the higher scores. A negatively skewed distribution is nonsymmetrical and has a distinct tail over the lower scores. A bimodal distribution is symmetrical and has two "humps" of equal height. A rectangular distribution is symmetrical, but has no distinct low-frequency tails.

6. A negatively skewed distribution indicates the test was relatively easy for most students. This is because most scores are middle or high scores and seldom are there relatively low scores.

7. It tells you that only 25% of all those who took the test scored better than you did. Therefore, you should feel pretty good about your intelligence score on this test.

8. a. It indicates the test is a difficult one, and many students get lower scores.
    b. It means you scored highly on the test, when few other students did so.

9. a. A score's simple frequency is how many times it occurred. Its relative frequency is the proportion of time it occurred.
    b. A score's cumulative frequency is the frequency of all scores occurring at or below the score. A score's percentile is the percentage of all scores occurring at or below the score.

10. a. You should put the scores into the left-hand column with the highest score in the data at the top of the column, followed by all possible scores in decreasing order down to the lowest score that has occurred.
    b. It should equal N.
    c. It should equal 1.00.
    d. It should equal N.

11. The proportion of the area under the curve to the left of a score reflects the proportion of all scores that are below that score. By multiplying this proportion by 100, we obtain the percentage of all scores below the score, which is the score's percentile.

12. a. 0 .13
    b. 0.50
    c. 0.37, because $0.50 - 0.13 = 0.37$
    d. C, B, D, A
    e. D, C, B, A

13. **Blood Type**   *f*

Blood Type	*f*
B	3
AB–	3
A–	2
O	7
A	5

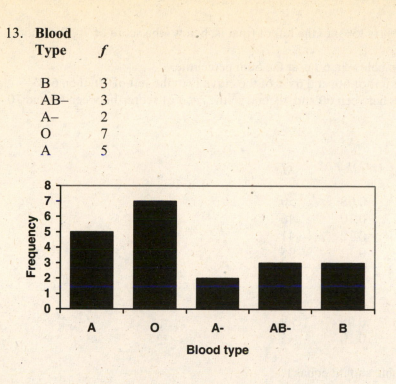

14. The distribution is best described as positively skewed.

15.

Scores	*f*	*rel. f*	*cf*
87	6	0.21	29
86	10	0.34	23
85	5	0.17	13
84	2	0.07	8
83	4	0.14	6
82	0	0.00	2
81	2	0.07	2

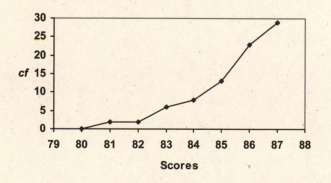

16. a. With 65% of the curve (100% − 35%) to the left of (that is, below) the score of 70, this score is at the 65th percentile.
    b. With 50% of the distribution below it, 60 is at the 50th percentile.
    c. If 50% of the curve is to the left of 60, and 65% of the curve is to the left of 70, then 65% − 50% = 15% of the curve lies between 60 and 70, and so the *rel. f* of scores between 60 and 70 is 0.15.

17. a.

Scores	*f*	*rel. f*	*cf*
25	4	0.08	50
24	5	0.10	46
23	6	0.12	41
22	6	0.12	35
21	8	0.16	29
20	7	0.14	21
19	5	0.10	14
18	4	0.08	9
17	5	0.10	5

  b. The sum of all *rel.f* in the table should equal 1.
  c. The highest *cf* should equal the *N* of 50.

18. a.

25	25	25	25	24	24	24	24	24	23	23	23
23	23	23	22	22	22	22	22	22	21	21	21
21	21	21	21	21	20	20	20	20	20	20	20
19	19	19	19	19	18	18	18	18	17	17	17
17	17										

  b. The distribution is approximately a normal curve.

ANSWERS TO THE TEST

1. d   2. c   3. a   4. b   5. b

Chapter 4
Measures of Central Tendency:
The Mean, Median, and Mode

YOU SHOULD LEARN

1. What measures of central tendency tell you.

2. What the mean, median, and mode are, and when each is used.

3. What deviations around the mean are, and why the sum of the deviations equals zero.

4. What a deviation tells us about a score's relative location and frequency in a normal distribution.

5. Why the sample mean is used to predict any score in the sample.

6. How to graph the results of an experiment and determine whether the graph reflects a relationship.

7. How each sample mean is used to estimate the population mean, and how a relationship in the population is described using μ.

YOU SHOULD LEARN WHEN, WHY, AND HOW TO USE THESE FORMULAS

1. The formula for computing the sample mean is

$$\overline{X} = \frac{\Sigma X}{N}$$

2. To estimate the median:

- Arrange the scores from lowest to highest.
- For an odd number of scores, the estimated median is the score in the middle position.
- For an even number of scores, the estimated median is the average of the two middle scores.

ONE MORE TIME: A Review

A score that summarizes the location of a distribution on a variable is called

a measure of _____ _____. The three common measures of | central tendency mean; median; mode | central tendency are the _____, _____, and _____. We

scale | decide which measure to use based on (1) the _____ used to

shape | measure the variable and (2) the _____ of the frequency distribution.

around | Other ways to think of central tendency include the score _____ which

typical; address | everyone scored, the _____ score, or the _____ for the

distribution as a whole.

The Mean, Median, and Mode

The measure of central tendency that is the most frequently occurring

mode | score in a distribution is called the _____. The mode is the preferred

nominal | measure when the scores involve a(n) _____ scale of measurement. A

distribution containing only one score having the highest frequency is called

unimodal | _____. A distribution containing two scores tied for the most

bimodal | frequently occurring score is called _____. The mode is possibly not

the most informative measure of central tendency because it does not take

scores | into account any _____ other than the most frequent score.

The measure of central tendency that is the score at the 50th percentile

median; Mdn | is the _____. The symbol for the median is _____. The median

ordinal | is the preferred measure when the data are from a(n) _____ scale. The

median also is used with interval and ratio data if the distribution is very

skewed; 50 | _____. On the normal curve, _____% of the area under the

left | curve lies to the _____ of the median. A problem with the median is

frequency | that it considers only the _____ of each score, and does not take into

value | account the _____ of each score.

The measure of central tendency located at the mathematical center of a

mean | distribution is the _____. The mean is used to describe data measured

using _____ or _____ scales. If the left half of the distribution	interval or ratio
mirrors the right half, the distribution is called _____. With	symmetrical
symmetrical distributions, most of the scores are located "_____" the	around
mean score. The ultimate symmetrical distribution is the _____	normal
distribution. To summarize a normal distribution, we should use the	
_____. In a normal distribution, the mean is at the 50th percentile.	mean
Therefore, the mean is also the _____. In a normal distribution, the	median
mean score is also the most frequently occurring score. Therefore, the mean	
is the _____.	mode
The mean does not accurately summarize a(n) _____ distribution.	skewed
In a positively skewed distribution, the mean is _____ than the	larger
median, and the median is _____ than the mode. In a negatively	larger
skewed distribution, the _____ has the smallest value, the _____	mean; mode
has the largest value, and the _____ falls between them. The most	median
accurate summary of a skewed distribution is usually the _____.	median
The symbol for a sample mean is _____. The formula for a	$\overline{X}$
sample mean is $\overline{X} =$ _____/_____. This indicates we should first find the	ΣX ; N
_____ of the scores and then divide by the _____ of scores. In	sum; number
words ΣX is the _____ _____ _____.	sum of X
When we transform raw scores using a constant, we use the symbol	
_____ to represent a constant. If we add K to every raw score, then the	K
mean of the transformed scores is the old mean _____ K. If we	plus
subtract K from every raw score, the new mean equals the old mean	
_____ K. Multiplying K times every raw score results in the new mean	minus

times

divided

being equal to the old mean _____ *K*. If every raw score is divided by

K, the new mean equals the old mean _____ *K*.

Deviations Around the Mean

The difference between a score and the mean is called the score's

deviation

$(X - \overline{X})$; larger

right

less

left

distance

_____. We calculate a score's deviation using the formula

_____. A positive deviation indicates the score is _____ than the

mean and so should be graphed to the _____ of the mean on a

frequency polygon. A negative deviation indicates the score is _____

than the mean and should be graphed to the _____ of the mean. The

size of the deviation (regardless of its sign) indicates the _____ the

score lies from the mean. A score that is equal to the mean has a deviation

0; farther

equal to _____. The larger the deviation, the _____ the score is

from the mean. On a normal distribution, the larger a deviation is (either

tail

frequency

positive or negative), the farther out in the _____ the score is and

hence, the lower the score's _____.

sum; around

$\Sigma(X - \overline{X})$

0

above; below

When we add together all the deviations in a sample, we find the

"_____ of the deviations _____ the mean." We indicate this in

statistical notation as _____. The sum of the deviations around the

mean always equals _____. This indicates that, in total, the mean is

just as far from the scores _____ it as it is from the scores _____

it.

Using the Mean to Predict and Interpret Scores

mean

When we don't know anything else about the scores, the _____ is our

best prediction about the score that any individual obtains. The difference

between a participant's actual score and the predicted score (the mean) is

symbolized by _____. The total error in predicting all scores in a	$(X - \overline{X})$
sample is equal to the _____ of the deviations. The total error in our	sum
prediction always equals _____.	$\Sigma(X - \overline{X})$

Describing the Population Mean

The Greek letter _____ is used to symbolize the population mean. Just	μ
as $\overline{X}$ is the best score to use when predicting any individual _____ in	score
a sample, the value of _____ is the best score to use when predicting	μ
any individual score in the _____. The formula for calculating the	population
population mean is _____ / _____, which is the same as the formula for the	ΣX; N
sample _____.	mean

Summarizing Research

In a correlational study, we often calculate the mean for the _____	X
variable and the _____ for the Y variable. Using this information, we	mean
can _____ the scores for other individuals within the population. For	predict
an experiment, we decide which measure of _____ _____ is	central tendency
appropriate based on the measurement scale of the _____ variable.	dependent
Oftentimes, the dependent variable is normally distributed, so we would	
want to compute the _____.	mean
In an experiment, we usually want to compute a separate mean for each	
_____ of the independent variable. We know a relationship exists if	condition
the means from at least two conditions are _____.	different

Graphing the Results of an Experiment

The results of an experiment are graphed by placing the independent variable	
on the _____ axis and the dependent variable on the _____ axis.	X; Y

conditions

mean

horizontal

dependent

independent

relationship

means

change; relationship

independent

line; straight

lines

bar; don't

The values on the X axis correspond to the _____ of the independent variable. The values on the Y axis usually correspond to the _____ in each condition. On a line graph, when the mean of the Y scores change as the conditions change, then the data points form a line that is not _____. This indicates that the scores on the _____ variable tend to change as a function of changes in the _____ variable, and thus that there is a(n) _____. If the data points form a horizontal line, then there are no differences between the _____ of the conditions. This indicates that the raw scores do not _____, and so there is no _____.

The type of graph we create is determined by the characteristics of the _____ variable. If it is an interval or ratio variable, we create a(n) _____ graph, in which we connect the data points with _____. If the independent variable is a nominal or ordinal variable, then we create a(n) _____ graph. In a bar graph, the bars _____ touch.

Inferring the Relationship in the Population

If we demonstrate a relationship in the sample data, then we want to infer that there is the same relationship in the _____. To do that, we must first perform the appropriate _____ statistical procedure. If the data pass the inferential test, then we assume that each sample of scores is _____ of the population of scores that would be found if we tested the population under that _____.

When we summarize a population using the mean, we assume that the population forms a(n) _____ distribution. The symbol for a population mean is _____. Our best estimate of the value of μ found under a

population

inferential

representative

condition

normal

μ

given condition is the value of _____ obtained under that condition. | $\overline{X}$

The ultimate goal of an experiment is to conclude that we would find

different populations of _____ having different values of _____ | scores; μ

as we changed the _____ of the independent variable. This would | conditions

allow us to conclude that there is a(n) _____ in the population. | relationship

Because a relationship in the population reflects the behavior of everyone of

interest, we would reach the scientist's goal of learning something about a(n)

_____ _____ _____. | law of nature

NOW DO YOU KNOW?

ΣX Mdn $\overline{X}$ K $X - \overline{X}$ $\Sigma(X - \overline{X})$ μ

measure of central tendency	mean
mode	deviation
unimodal distribution	sum of deviations around the mean
bimodal distribution	line graph
median	bar graph

USING WHAT YOU KNOW

1. a. What do measures of central tendency tell us about a distribution of scores?
   b. What are the three most common measures of central tendency?
   c. What two aspects of the data determine which measure of central tendency to use?

2. Why is the mean the best measure of central tendency for a normal distribution?

3. Why is the mean an inappropriate measure of central tendency in a very skewed distribution?

4. What two problems can arise when using the mode to describe central tendency?

5. When the mean, the median, and the mode of a distribution have the same value, what does it tell you about the distribution?

6. The following distribution shows the locations of five scores:

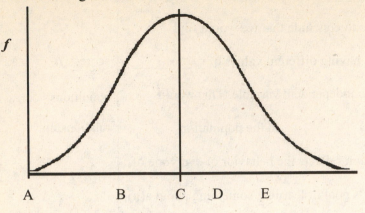

   A   B   C   D   E

   a. Match the deviation scores –7, +1, 0, –2, and +5 with their locations.
      A = _____   B = _____   C = _____   D = _____   E = _____
   b. Rank-order the deviation scores to show the order of the raw scores from highest to lowest.
   c. Rank-order the deviation scores to show the order of the raw scores from highest frequency to lowest frequency.

7. a. What does $\Sigma(X - \overline{X})$ mean?
   b. What two steps are performed in finding $\Sigma(X - \overline{X})$?
   c. What value does $\Sigma(X - \overline{X})$ *always* equal?

8. a. What is μ?
   b. What are four characteristics of μ?

9. What two assumptions must be made in order to use a sample mean to estimate μ?

10. A researcher collected several sets of data. For each, indicate which measure of central tendency she should compute.

    a. The following personality scores:
           0, 2, 3, 3, 8, 4, 9, 6, 7, 5, 6
    b. The following age scores:
           10, 15, 18, 15, 14, 13, 42, 15, 12, 14, 42
    c. The following college years:
           freshman, senior, junior, junior, freshman, freshman, junior, sophomore, junior
    d. The following political affiliations:
           Dem., Dem., Rep., Dem., Soc., Com., Com., Soc., Dem., Rep.

11. For each of the four sets of data in problem 10 indicate whether a line graph or a bar graph would be appropriate and why.

12. a. When graphing the results of an experiment, what is plotted on the Y axis?
    b. What determines the measure of central tendency you should plot?

13. For each of the graphs pictured, what do you conclude about
    a. the $\overline{X}$ in each condition?
    b. the scores in each condition?
    c. the population mean in each condition?
    d. the relationship in the population?

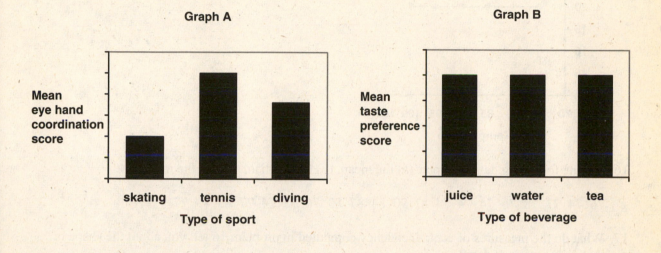

14. Does Graph C indicate a relationship? Why or why not?

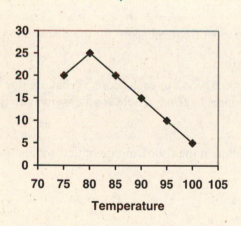

15. Does Graph D indicate a relationship? Why or why not?

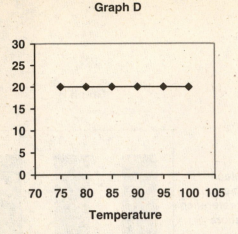

16. For the following data, compute (a) the mean, (b) the median, and (c) the mode:

    76 74 73 78 76 74 74 74 81 90 84 87 83 76 75 74 77 83 89 77

17. What do the measures of central tendency computed in problem 16 tell you about the shape of that distribution of data?

18. Which measure of central tendency most accurately summarizes the distribution of scores in problem 16?

19. Which measure of central tendency best describes the most frequent score for the distribution in problem 16?

20. We transform the scores in problem 16 by adding 2,000.519642 to each score. What are the mean, the median, and the mode of the transformed scores? (*Hint:* There is an easy way to do this!)

21. In a normal distribution of scores four participants obtained the following deviation scores: −1, +2, +3, and −0.15.

    a. Which participant obtained the highest raw score?
    b. Which participant obtained the lowest raw score?
    c. Rank-order the deviation scores in terms of their frequency, putting the score with the highest frequency first.

22. If the median of a distribution is considerably greater than the mean, what do you know about the shape of the distribution?

23. Why do we use the mean to predict a person's score on a variable when we have no other information?

THE TEST

1. The first step in summarizing any set of data into one number by

    a. writing out each score.
    b. finding the relative and cumulative frequencies of each score.
    c. calculating N.
    d. computing the appropriate measure of central tendency.

2. Which measure of central tendency is preferred for describing interval or ratio data in a highly skewed distribution?

    a. the mode.
    b. the median.
    c. the mean.
    d. either the mean or the mode.

3. When you do not know anything else about the scores, the mean is the best score to use when describing or predicting any individual's score because in the long run your total error will be

    a. zero.
    b. equal to the sum of the raw scores.
    c. equal to N times the mean.
    d. a negative value.

4. You have subtracted the mean from each score in a sample that is approximately normally distributed. Which of the following deviation scores is likely to have the highest frequency?

    a. −12
    b. −7
    c. +2
    d. +18

5. In a line graph summarizing the results of an experiment, the absence of a relationship would be shown by which of the following?

    a. a line going sharply upward from left to right.
    b. a line going sharply downward from left to right.
    c. a line going sharply up and then sharply down.
    d. a horizontal line from left to right.

ANSWERS TO USING WHAT YOU KNOW

1. a.   They indicate where most of the scores in a distribution are located.
    b.   The mean, median, and mode.
    c.   The type of measurement scale and, for interval and ratio scores, the shape of the distribution.

2. Because the mean is the score at the mathematical center, and for a normal distribution, that is where most of the scores are.

3. Because the mean, at the mathematical center of the distribution, is not located near most of the scores.

4. There may be many scores that qualify as the mode; most of the scores may not be located around the mode.

5. The distribution is a perfect normal distribution.

6. a. $A = -7, B = -2, C = 0, D = +1, E = +5$
    b. $+5, +1, 0, -2, -7$
    c. $0, +1, -2, +5, -7$

7. a. $\Sigma(X - \overline{X})$ is the sum of the deviations around the mean.
    b.   First, the mean is subtracted from each score in the distribution to obtain the deviations around the mean. Then, these deviations are summed (added).
    c.   The sum of the deviations around the mean must always equal 0.
8. a. μ is the symbol for the mean of a population of scores.
    b. μ is the average score in the population; μ is the center of the distribution; the sum of the deviations around μ equals 0; and μ is the predicted score for each subject in the population.

9. The population is at least approximately normally distributed, and the sample is representative of the population.

10. a.   Mean (this is an interval variable).
    b.   Median (these ratio scores are skewed).
    c.   Median (this is an ordinal variable).
    d.   Mode (this is a nominal variable).

11. a.   A line graph because the data are interval.
    b.   A line graph because the data are ratio.
    c.   A bar graph because the data are ordinal.
    d.   A bar graph because the data are nominal.

12. a.   The measure of central tendency of the dependent scores in each condition.
    b.   The scale of measurement and the shape of the distribution of the dependent variable.

13. Graph A: a. the means are different; b. the scores tend to be different; c. the μs differ; d. there is a relationship.
Graph B: a. the means do not differ; b. the scores do not differ; c. the μs do not differ; d. there is no relationship.

14. Yes, because the number of units completed changes as a function of room temperature. The summary data points do not form a horizontal line.

15. No, because the summary data points form a horizontal line.

16. a. $\Sigma X = 1575$, $N = 20$, $\overline{X} = 78.75$.
    b.   Averaging 76 and 77 (the scores in positions 10 and 11 out of the 20) gives an estimated median of 76.5.
    c.   Mode = 74.

17. Because the mean is larger than the median, which is larger than the mode, this is a positively skewed distribution.

18. Median.

19. This is a trick question: The mode is the most frequent score.

20. Add the constant to the original measures found in problem 16: $\overline{X} = 2{,}079.269642$, Mdn = $2{,}077.019642$, mode = $2{,}074.519642$.

21. a.   The participant who obtained the +3 deviation.
    b.   The participant who obtained the −1 deviation.
    c.   −0.15, −1, +2, +3

22. The distribution is severely negatively skewed.

23. Because over the long run, overestimates and underestimates from such predictions will cancel out. Mathematically, the total error is the sum of the deviations, or $\Sigma(X - \overline{X})$ which equals 0.

ANSWERS TO THE TEST

1. d   2. b   3. a   4. c   5. d

Chapter 5
Measures of Variability:
Range, Variance, and Standard Deviation

YOU SHOULD LEARN

1. What is meant by variability.

2. When the range is used and how to interpret it.

3. When the sample variance and standard deviation are used, and how to interpret them.

4. Why we use the unbiased estimators of the population variance and standard deviation, and how to interpret them.

5. How the standard deviation helps to describe a normal distribution.

6. How variance is used to measure errors in prediction, and what is meant by the proportion of variance accounted for.

YOU SHOULD LEARN WHEN, WHY, AND HOW TO USE THESE FORMULAS

1. The formula for the range is

    Range = Highest score – Lowest score

2. The computational formulas for the variance are

Sample Variance	Estimated Population Variance

    $$S_X^2 = \dfrac{\Sigma X^2 - \dfrac{(\Sigma X)^2}{N}}{N} \qquad\qquad s_X^2 = \dfrac{\Sigma X^2 - \dfrac{(\Sigma X)^2}{N}}{N-1}$$

3. The computational formulas for the standard deviation are

Sample Standard Deviation	Estimated Population Standard Deviation

    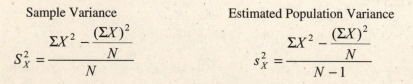

    $$S_X = \sqrt{\dfrac{\Sigma X^2 - \dfrac{(\Sigma X)^2}{N}}{N}} \qquad\qquad s_X = \sqrt{\dfrac{\Sigma X^2 - \dfrac{(\Sigma X)^2}{N}}{N-1}}$$

ONE MORE TIME: A Review

Statistics that communicate the extent to which scores are different from one another are called measures of _____. The greater the variability, the _____ the scores are spread out, and thus the _____ accurately they are represented by the measure of central tendency.

variability

more; less

The Range

The measure of variability that indicates how far the lowest score is from the highest score is the _____. We usually use the range as the only measure of variability with _____ or _____ data. With nominal data, the range is the number of _____. With ordinal data, we find the range by taking the _____ between the lowest and highest rank. For interval or ratio data, the range is computed using the formula _____ score _____ lowest score.

range

nominal or ordinal

categories

difference

highest

minus

Understanding The Variance and Standard Deviation

When the mean is the appropriate measure of central tendency, we use the two measures of variability called the _____ and the _____ _____. The smaller the variance and standard deviation, the _____ the scores are spread out around the mean, and thus the _____ the scores differ from one another.

variance; standard

deviation

less

less

Although there is a better computational formula, to understand the variance, we first find the amount that each score _____ from the mean, which is symbolized as the quantity _____. Then, we _____ each deviation and find the sum. In symbols, this is the quantity _____. Next, we divide this sum by _____, which is the number of _____.

deviates

$(X - \overline{X})$

square

$\Sigma(X - \overline{X})^2$; N

deviations (scores)

square root	To find the standard deviation, we must take the _____ _____ of the variance.
	The variance and standard deviation tell us the amount the scores are
above; below	spread out _____ and _____ the mean. Thus, when many of the scores are spread out over a relatively wide range, the standard deviation and
large	variance will be relatively _____. To describe where most of the scores above and below the mean are located, we find the score at
plus	_____ one standard deviation from the mean and the score at
minus	_____ one standard deviation from the mean. In symbols, these scores
$+1S_X$; $-1S_X$	lie at _____ and _____ from the mean. In a perfectly normal
34	distribution, approximately _____% of all scores fall between the mean and the score that is one standard deviation from the mean. Therefore,
68	approximately _____% of the scores in the distribution lie between the score at $+1S_X$ from the mean and the score at $-1S_X$ from the mean.

Computing the Sample Variance and Sample Standard Deviation

S_X^2	The symbol for the sample variance is _____. In the computational
ΣX	formula for S_X^2, we first find the sum of X, symbolized as _____, and
$(\Sigma X)^2$	then we square the sum of X, symbolized as _____. We must also find
ΣX^2	the sum of the squared Xs, symbolized as _____. This symbol tells us
square; add	to first _____ the X scores, and then _____ them. To find the
$(\Sigma X)^2$	variance, we first divide the quantity _____ by N. We then subtract
ΣX^2	that answer from the quantity _____. Finally, we divide the difference
N; relative	by _____. The variance communicates the _____ variability of the scores. However, the variance can be difficult to interpret, because it is
squared	measured in _____ units.

The measure of variability that more directly relates to the average

deviation of the raw scores is the _____ _____. Mathematically,   standard deviation

the standard deviation equals the _____ _____ of the variance.   square root

Conversely, the _____ of the standard deviation is the _____.   square; variance

The symbol for the sample standard deviation is _____. The S_X

computational formula for S_X requires adding the symbol for _____   square

_____ to the computational formula for the _____. The value of   root ; variance

S_X can be thought of as the "average" of the _____ from the   deviations

_____. For a normal distribution, the standard deviation should be   mean

approximately _____ of the range.   one-sixth

The Population Variance and Standard Deviation

The symbol for the true population standard deviation is _____, and σ_X

the symbol for the true population variance is _____. Both are ways of σ_X^2

summarizing how much the scores differ from _____. Most often, we μ

must _____ the values of these population parameters based on a   estimate

sample. To do this, however, we do not use the formulas for _____ S_X

and _____ because they are biased estimators. They are biased toward S_X^2

_____ the true population standard deviation and variance. This is   underestimating

because, of the _____ scores in a sample, only _____ of them $N; N-1$

actually reflect the variability in the population. If we estimate the

population variability using the formulas for the sample, we are dividing by

too _____ a number, and so the answer tends to be too _____.   large; small

To estimate the variability in the population, we compute the

_____ estimators of the population parameters. The symbol for the   unbiased

s_X

unbiased estimator of the population standard deviation is _____, and the symbol for the unbiased estimator of the population variance is

s_X^2

_____. The computational formulas for the unbiased estimators are the same as the corresponding formulas for a sample, except that in s_X^2 and s_X,

$N - 1$

the final division involves dividing by _____. The quantity $N - 1$ is

degrees of freedom

called the _____ _____ _____. The symbol for degrees of

df

freedom is _____. We compute s_X^2 and s_X using the scores from a(n)

sample

_____, but they are our best estimates of the values we would find if

σ_X^2 ; σ_X

we computed _____ and _____, respectively. We expect about

$+1s_X$

68% of a normal distribution to fall between the scores at _____ and

$-1s_X$

_____ from μ.

     When we conduct an experiment, we should compute both the mean and

condition

the standard deviation for each _____. In this way, we know if the

consistent

scores are more or less _____ in each condition.

Variability and the Strength of a Relationship

When the variability among scores as measured by the standard deviation is

strong

low, we know the overall relationship is _____. This is because a

consistent

stronger relationship is more _____. On the other hand, if our standard

weak

deviation is high, then our relationship is _____.

Variability and Errors in Prediction

mean

If we have no other information about unknown scores, then the _____

is the best score to use to predict them. The amount of error in our

variability

predictions is determined by the amount of _____ in the scores.

This is because the greater the variability, the _____ the differences	greater
between the mean and the scores, and thus, the _____ our error when	greater
we use the mean to predict the scores. So _____ and _____ can	S_X ; S_X^2
be viewed as the _____ error we have when using the sample mean to	average
predict scores in a sample.	

Accounting for Variance

When we compute the variance of all the Y variable scores in a study, we	
have determined the variance we need to _____ _____. In a	account for
strong relationship, the independent variable _____ for most of the	accounts
variance in the dependent variable. When the relationship is week, however,	
the independent variable does not account for much of the _____ in	variance
the dependent variable.	

NOW DO YOU KNOW?

ΣX ΣX^2 $(\Sigma X)^2$ S_X^2 S_X σ_X^2 σ_X s_X^2 s_X $N-1$ df

sum of the squared Xs	population variance
squared sum of X	biased estimators
measures of variability	unbiased estimators
range	estimated population standard deviation
sample variance	estimated population variance
sample standard deviation	degrees of freedom
population standard deviation	proportion of variance accounted for

USING WHAT YOU KNOW

1. What two characteristics of a distribution are needed in order to accurately describe the distribution?

2. a. What information do measures of variability convey?
   b. Why is a measure of central tendency a less accurate description of a distribution if the measure of variability is large?

3. a. Distinguish among the symbols "S," "σ," and "s."
    b. When are the above symbols accompanied by the squared sign (^{2})?

4. a. With what type(s) of data should the range be used?
    b. With what type(s) of data should the variance and standard deviation be used?

5. a. What do both the variance and the standard deviation indicate about a distribution of data?
    b. To describe the variability of a distribution, which should usually be employed—the standard deviation or the variance? Why?

6. For the following set of scores, calculate the range, the sample mean ($\overline{X}$), the sample variance (S_X^2), and the sample standard deviation (S_X).

    23 25 17 19 21 20 22 20 24 23 21 19 20 17 25 23 19 20 22 22

7. a. Compute the estimated population variance (s_X^2) and the estimated population standard deviation (s_X) for the sample in problem 6.
    b. Why are the numbers computed here larger than those computed in problem 6?
    c. Why must the estimates be computed this way?

8. For a distribution with a mean of 130 and a standard deviation of 15, approximately 68% of the scores will lie between which two scores?

9. Suppose you want to estimate population parameters from a sample of 30 scores. You decide to use the sample mean to estimate the population mean, and then you estimate the population variance as

$$S_X^2 = \frac{740 - \frac{(112)^2}{30}}{30} = 10.729$$

    a. What did you do wrong?
    b. What should your estimate be?

10. If a distribution has a large variance, why are our predictions about scores in that distribution inaccurate?

11. Name three things the standard deviation and variance tell us.

12. A researcher obtains $S_X = 7.3$ and $S_X^2 = 53.29$. He then decides to transform the scores by adding 5 to each score.

    a. What are the values of the standard deviation and variance after this transformation?
    b. He then decides to transform the scores by dividing each score by $K = 10$. What will be the values of the standard deviation and variance after this transformation?

13. If the variance of 10 scores is computed as follows:

$$\sqrt{\frac{40 - \frac{(16)^2}{10}}{10}} = 1.20$$

And the standard deviation is then computed as follows:

$$\frac{40 - \frac{(16)^2}{10}}{10} = 1.44$$

   a.   What is the problem here?
   b.   What is it about the answers that should have alerted you that something was wrong?

14. You first compute the sample variance as

$$\frac{392 - \frac{(55)^2}{10}}{9} = 9.94$$

Then you compute the estimated population variance as

$$\frac{392 - \frac{(55)^2}{10}}{10} = 8.95$$

   a.   What is the problem here?
   b.   What is it about these answers that should have alerted you that something was wrong?

15. The new statistician for the football team at the Institute of Psycho-Ceramics has calculated the following player statistics. Player A's average rushing yards per carry is $\overline{X} = 5$ with a standard deviation of 3; Player B's average rushing yards per carry is $\overline{X} = 5$ with a standard deviation of 10.

   a.   Which player is the more consistent yardage gainer? Why?
   b.   Which player is more likely to break loose for a big run? Why?

16. For the data set in problem 6 what is the sample variance (S_X^2) if you add 5 to each score?

17. When summarizing data, what three things do the standard deviation and variance indicate?

18. A teacher finds that for test grades in Class A, $\overline{X} = 32$ and $S_X = 4$; for test grades in Class B, $\overline{X} = 32$ and $S_X = 8$.

   a.   What score should he predict for students in each class?
   b.   Which class permits the better predictions? Why?

19. For the data in problem 18, the teacher discovers that test grades are related to the amount of time that students study; hence, he uses the amount of study time to predict each student's test grade.

    a.   By using this relationship, he finds that he can account for 50% of the variance in test grades in A. What does this mean?

    b.   The relationship accounts for 63% of the variance in Class B. In which class is the relationship more useful? Why?

THE TEST

1. In general, with fairly normal distributions measured with interval or ratio scales, which measure of variability is best?

    a.   The range.
    b.   The mean.
    c.   The variance.
    d.   The median.

2. When using the sample variance to estimate the population variance in an inferential situation, what must you do so that your estimate is not biased?

    a.   Use large samples.
    b.   Be sure selection is random.
    c.   Use the total number of scores (N) in the final division.
    d.   Use the degrees of freedom ($N - 1$) in the final division.

3. Which of the following is not indicated by the standard deviation?

    a.   The consistency in the scores.
    b.   The location of the middle of the distribution.
    c.   How far the scores are spread out around the mean.
    d.   The "average deviation" from the mean.

4. The advantage to using the standard deviation rather than the variance as a measure of variability is that

    a.   variance is an inaccurate measure.
    b.   variance does not take into account the most extreme scores.
    c.   the standard deviation underestimates less.
    d.   the standard deviation is easier to interpret.

5. The stronger and more consistent a relationship,

    a.   the less the proportion of variance that is accounted for.
    b.   the greater the proportion of variance that is accounted for.
    c.   nothing can be inferred about the proportion of variance accounted for.
    d.   the more error we must tolerate.

ANSWERS TO USING WHAT YOU KNOW

1. A measure of central tendency and a measure of variability.

2. a. They convey the extent to which scores differ or are spread out, usually in relation to the mean.
   b. The greater the variability, the more the scores are spread out; thus, the location of the distribution is less accurately described by the one score that is the measure of central tendency.

3. a. S indicates a sample statistic that describes the sample; σ indicates a true population parameter that describes the population; and s indicates an estimate of the population parameter computed from a sample.
   b. When "^{2}" is present, the symbol indicates a variance; when "^{2}" is not present, the symbol indicates a standard deviation.

4. a. Nominal or ordinal data.
   b. Interval or ratio data forming a normal distribution.

5. a. They are both ways to describe the variability or spread of the scores around the mean.
   b. The standard deviation. It measures in the same units as the raw scores, and so it more directly indicates the "average" deviation of the scores from the mean. It also can be applied directly to the normal curve.

6. Range $= 25 - 17 = 8$; $\overline{X} = 21.10$; $S_X^2 = 5.19$; $S_X = 2.28$.

7. a. $s_X^2 = 5.46$; $s_X = 2.34$.
   b. Because the final division here is by $N - 1$, which results in a larger answer.
   c. Of the N scores in a sample, only $N - 1$ of them reflect the variability in the population. Thus, to find the "average" of this variability, we divide by $N - 1$.

8. Between 115 $(130 - 15)$ and 145 $(130 + 15)$.

9. a. You computed the sample variance instead of the unbiased estimator.
   b. With a final division of 29 instead of 30, $s_X^2 = 11.099$.

10. Since we predict the mean score, a large variance indicates that the scores are relatively distant from the mean. Thus, our predictions are not close to the actual scores.

11. The standard deviation and variance tell us (a) how consistent the scores are, (b) the strength of the relationship, and (c) the "average error" when using the mean to predict scores.

12. a. They will be the same as before the transformation: $S_X = 7.3$, $S_X^2 = 53.29$.
    b. The new $S_X = 7.3/10 = 0.73$; the new S_X^2 is the square of the new S_X, or $0.73^2 = 0.53$.

13. a. The formula for standard deviation was used when computing variance and vice versa.
    b. The standard deviation is always smaller than the variance.

14. a. You have used the formula for the unbiased estimator to describe the sample and the formula for the sample variance to estimate the population.

    b. The estimated variance is always larger than the sample variance (and s_X is larger than S_X).

15. a. Player A: most of his runs are closer to his mean.

    b. Player B: his runs are more variable, covering a wider range of distances and presumably including some big gainers.

16. The answer is still $S_X^2 = 5.19$, because adding a constant does not change the variance.

17. The standard deviation and the variance indicate the consistency of the scores and behavior, the strength of the relationship, and the average error when using the mean to predict scores.

18. a. The mean, 32.

    b. Class A. The standard deviation is smaller. Therefore, the scores in that class are closer to the mean.

19. a. On average, he is 50% closer to predicting students' scores when he knows how long they study than if he merely predicts a score of 32 for them.

    b. Class B. Amount of study time allows him to more accurately predict the students' behavior on the test.

ANSWERS TO THE TEST

    1. c   2. d   3. b   4. d   5. b

Chapter 6
z-Scores and the Normal Curve Model

YOU SHOULD LEARN

1. What a z-score is and what it tells you about a score's relative location.

2. The characteristics of the z-distribution.

3. How the z-distribution is used to compare different distributions.

4. How the standard normal curve is used in conjunction with z-scores to determine the expected relative frequency, simple frequency, and percentile of scores.

5. The characteristics of a sampling distribution of means.

6. What is meant by the standard error of the mean.

7. How a sampling distribution of means is used with z-scores to determine the expected relative frequency of sample means.

YOU SHOULD LEARN WHEN, WHY, AND HOW TO USE THESE FORMULAS

1. The formula for transforming a raw score to a z-score is

$$z = \frac{X - \overline{X}}{S_X}$$

2. The formula for transforming a z-score to a raw score is

$$X = (z)(S_X) + \overline{X}$$

3. The formula for the true standard error of the mean is

$$\sigma_{\overline{X}} = \frac{\sigma_X}{\sqrt{N}}$$

4. The formula for transforming a sample mean to a z-score is

$$z = \frac{\overline{X} - \mu}{\sigma_{\overline{X}}}$$

ONE MORE TIME: A Review

When we evaluate one score relative to the sample or population in which

relative standing

the score occurs, we are describing the score's _____ _____. To

z-score

accomplish this, we compute the score's _____. A z-score indicates

deviates; mean

the amount that a score _____ from the _____ when measured in

standard deviation; z

_____ _____ units. The symbol for a z-score is _____.

The formula for transforming a raw score in a sample to a z-score is z =

$X; \overline{X} ; S_X$

(_____ – _____)/_____. According to this formula, we first subtract the

mean; score

_____ from the _____. We then divide this deviation by the

sample

_____ standard deviation, which is computed using the formula in

N

which the final division involves the quantity _____.

larger

A positive z-score indicates that the raw score is _____ than the

right

mean and graphed to the _____ of it. A negative z-score indicates that

smaller; left

the raw score is _____ than the mean and graphed to the _____

sign

of it. The absolute value of the z-score (ignoring the _____ of the

distance

score) indicates the _____ the raw score is from the mean. The z-score

0

for a score equal to the mean is _____. The larger a positive z-score,

larger

the _____ the value of the raw score. The larger the absolute value of a

smaller

negative z-score, the _____ the value of the raw score. In a normal

3

distribution, z-scores seldom are greater than plus or minus _____,

±3

which is symbolized as _____.

The absolute size of a z-score is based on both the size of the raw

deviation; standard

score's _____ from the mean and the size of the _____

deviation

_____. When the variability of the raw scores is large, a particular

small

deviation will produce a relatively _____ z-score. If our goal is to produce a large z-score, then we want a(n) _____ deviation and a(n) | large

_____ standard deviation. Since a z-score is a score, it describes a raw | small

score's _____ in terms of how far _____ or _____ the mean | location; above; below

it is. It also, however, indicates its _____ from the mean. | distance

    To transform a z-score to its corresponding raw score, we use the formula

_____ = (_____)(_____) + _____. | X; z; S_X; $\overline{X}$

The z-Distribution

Transforming an entire raw score distribution to z-scores results in a(n)

_____. Creating a z-distribution does not change the _____ of the | z-distribution; shape

distribution. Every z-distribution has a mean equal to _____. This is | 0

because the formula tells us to find the quantity _____. Whenever X | $(X - \overline{X})$

equals the mean, this quantity equals 0. Also, the standard deviation of every z-

distribution equals _____. Whether we are using a raw score or a z-score, | 1

the _____ location on the distribution is the same. | relative

    One reason to transform raw scores to z-scores is to make scores from

_____ variables comparable. Comparing z-scores allows us to compare | different

participants' scores based on their _____ _____ in each sample. | relative standing

Also, different z-distributions can be plotted on _____ graph(s). | one

    Another reason to compute z-scores is to determine the _____ | relative

frequency of raw scores. This is particularly relevant when the scores form a(n)

_____ distribution. From the graph of a normal distribution, the larger the | normal

absolute value of z, the _____ into the tail of the distribution the z-score | farther

lies; therefore, the _____ its frequency. The larger the absolute size of the | lower

z-score, the _____ the frequency of the corresponding raw score. | lower

sample	A third use of *z*-scores is to describe and interpret _____
means; relative standing	_____. This allows us to determine the _____ _____ of an
mean	entire sample by evaluating its sample _____ in comparison to means
compare	of other samples. So the three main uses of *z*-scores are (1) to _____
	scores from two or more variables, (2) to determine the relative frequencies
raw; samples	of _____ scores, and (3) to see how multiple _____ from the
	same population compare to each other.

Using the z-Distribution to Determine Relative Frequency

proportion	Relative frequency is the _____ of time that a score occurs, and we
area	can compute it as the proportion of the total _____ under the
normal	_____ curve. Our model of any normal *z*-distribution is the
standard	_____ normal curve. The standard normal curve model is appropriate
approximately	if the data are at least _____ normally distributed.
	To use the standard normal curve model, we first transform the raw
z-score	score to a(n) _____. Then, from the standard normal curve, we
proportion	determine the _____ of the total area under the curve above or below
z-table	the *z*-score. Normal curve areas are listed in the _____ located in the
relative	appendix of the textbook. Each proportion equals the _____
frequency	_____ of the corresponding *z*-scores on a perfect normal curve. It is
raw scores	also the relative frequency of the corresponding _____ _____ on
	a perfect normal distribution.
	A score's expected percentile is the percentage of all scores that are
less; left	_____ than and graphed to the _____ of the score. When
	computing the percentile of a score having a positive *z*-score, we consult the
score	table to obtain the proportion of scores between the _____ and the

_____. Then we must add _____ to this proportion so that we have | mean; 0.50

the proportion of all scores below the score. The percentile of a score having a

negative z-score corresponds to the proportion of scores from the table located

_____ the z-score. | beyond

Using the Standard Normal Curve to Describe Sample Means

We also use z-scores to describe a sample mean using the _____ of all | distribution

means. This distribution is called the _____ distribution of _____. | sampling; means

The sampling distribution of means is the distribution of all possible sample

means that can be _____ obtained from one particular population of | randomly

_____ _____ all with the same size _____. The different | raw scores; N

values of X in a sampling distribution occur simply by the luck of the draw of

the particular _____ that were selected. | scores

The sampling distribution of means forms a(n) _____ _____, | normal distribution

and the mean of the sampling distribution equals the _____ of the raw | mean

score population, which is symbolized as _____. Also, the larger the | μ

differences among the raw scores, the _____ the differences among the | larger

sample means. Conversely, if the raw scores are not spread out, then there is

little _____ in the sample means. | variability

To describe the variability in the sampling distribution of means, we

compute the _____ _____ of the _____. The standard error of | standard error; mean

the mean is the _____ _____ of the sampling distribution of means. | standard deviation

The symbol for the true standard error of the mean is _____. The formula | $\sigma_{\bar{X}}$

for the true standard error of the mean is $\sigma_{\bar{X}} = $ _____ / _____. The σ_X in the | σ_X ; $\sqrt{N}$

formula stands for the _____ standard deviation of the population of | true

_____ _____, and N is the number of scores used to compute each | raw scores

mean	_____ in the sampling distribution. N is also the number of scores in
sample	the _____ for which we are computing the z-score.

Computing a z-Score for a Sample Mean

To determine a mean's relative location on a sampling distribution, we

z-score	transform the sample mean into a(n) _____. The formula for
$\overline{X}; \mu; \sigma_{\overline{X}}$	transforming a sample mean into a z-score is $z = ($ _____ $-$ _____ $) /$ _____.
sampling	The symbol μ stands for the mean of the _____ distribution, which is
μ	equal to the raw score _____. Then the z-score indicates the amount
$\overline{X}; \mu$	that a given _____ deviates from _____ when measured in
standard error	_____ _____ units. A sample mean will have a large z-score
large	when the difference between $\overline{X}$ and μ is _____ and/or the variability
small	as measured by σ_X is _____.

	Once we have calculated the z-score for a sample mean, we can use the
standard normal; proportion	_____ _____ curve to determine the _____ of the area
	under the curve. Whenever you are using z-scores, you should always draw
normal; mean	the _____ curve. You should label the raw score _____ and the
raw	approximate location of a given _____ score and its associated
z-score	_____.

NOW DO YOU KNOW?

z $\pm$ $\sigma_{\overline{X}}$

relative standing   standard normal curve
z-score   sampling distribution of means
z-distribution   central limit theorem
standard scores   standard error of the mean

USING WHAT YOU KNOW

1. a. What does a z-score transformation tell you?
    b. What factors determine the absolute value of the z-score?

2. Describe the mean, standard deviation, and shape of the z-distribution.

3. Why are z-scores referred to as standard scores?

4. a. What is the standard normal curve model?
    b. What is it used for?
    c. What criteria should be met for the model to give an accurate description of a sample?

5. Dr. Jones has administered a test to her students. She calculated a $\overline{X} = 86$ and $S_X = 12$.

    a. What is the z-score of a student with a raw score of 80?
    b. What is the z-score of a student with a raw score of 98?
    c. What is the raw score for a student with a z-score of -1.5?
    d. What is the raw score for a student with a z-score of $+1.0$?

6. Which z-score corresponds to the smaller raw score in each of the following pairs?

    a. $z = -2.8$ and $z = -1.7$
    b. $z = +1.0$ and $z = +2.3$
    c. $z = -0.7$ and $z = +1.5$
    d. $z = 0$ and $z = -1.9$

7. In problem 6, which z-score in each pair has the higher frequency?

8. If a set of scores has a sample mean of 25 and a sample variance of 4, find the following:

    a. The z-score for a raw score of 31.
    b. The z-score for a raw score of 18.
    c. The raw score for a z-score of -2.5.
    d. The raw score for a z-score of $+0.5$.

9. Of the z-scores -2.3, $+1.0$, $+0.9$, and -0.6,

    a. which z-score corresponds to the smallest raw score?
    b. which z-score reflects the raw score having the highest frequency?

10. What proportion of the area under the standard normal curve would you expect to be

    a. between $z = -1.2$ and $z = + 0.6$?
    b. below $z = 1.4$?
    c. below $z = -2.6$?
    d. above $z = -2.0$?

11. Suppose you have two normal distributions containing different scores and different ranges.

    a. If you want to know the relative frequency of scores above $z = +0.97$ for each distribution, what should you do?

    b. If you also want to know the expected relative frequency of scores between the $\overline{X}$ and 100 for each distribution, what should you do?

12. Find the relative frequency of scores

    a. between the mean and $z = +1.40$.

    b. below $z = -1.86$.

    c. above $z = +2.68$.

    d. below $z = -2.4$ and above $z = +1.96$.

13. For a distribution in which the mean is 100 and the standard deviation is 12, find the following:

    a. the relative frequency of scores between 76 and the mean.

    b. the relative frequency of scores above 112.

    c. the percentile of a score of 106.

    d. the percentile of a score of 84.

14. In problem 13, $N = 700$.

    a. How many participants are expected to score between 76 and 100?

    b. How many are expected to score above 112?

15. a. What are the shape, mean, and standard deviation of a sampling distribution of means?

    b. What does that sampling distribution of means reflect?

16. In the population, the average score on a test of self-esteem is 50 ($\sigma = 5$). You select a random sample of 25 students who score a mean of 53.

    a. Sally claims that these students don't have very high self-esteem, because they are only 3 points above the population mean. Why can't she make this claim merely by looking at the X?

    b. What should she do?

    c. What is the z-score for this sample?

    d. What conclusion do you draw about your sample?

17. A researcher investigates the speed with which a random sample of 50 participants completes an analogies test. She obtains a sample mean of 136.42 minutes. For the population of people who have taken this test, the mean is 130 and the standard deviation is 18.

    a. What percentage of the time can she expect to obtain a sample mean of 136.42 or above?

    b. Explain why she obtained such an unusual $\overline{X}$.

THE TEST

1. A *z*-score is an indicator of how much a score deviates from the

   a. mean in raw score units.
   b. median in percentage units.
   c. mean in standard deviation units.
   d. other scores in percentage units.

2. If you know a *z*-score and you want to compute the corresponding raw score, you would first _____ and then _____.

   a. multiply the *z*-score by the standard deviation; add the mean
   b. multiply the *z*-score by the mean; add the standard deviation
   c. add the mean to the *z*-score; multiply the result by the standard deviation
   d. add the standard deviation to the *z*-score; multiply the result by the mean

3. In any normal distribution, *z*-scores between +1 and –1 occur approximately _____% of the time.

   a. 34
   b. 50
   c. 68
   d. 95

4. The mean of the sampling distribution of sample means will always equal

   a. the sample mean.
   b. the population mean.
   c. the sample mean divided by the square root of *N*.
   d. the population mean divided by the square root of *N*.

5. The standard deviation of the sampling distribution of means is called the

   a. standard deviation.
   b. standard error of the mean.
   c. *z*-score.
   d. standard normal curve.

ANSWERS TO USING WHAT YOU KNOW

1. a. *z* indicates how far a score is from the mean when measured in standard deviation units.
   b. The size of the raw score's deviation and the size of S_X.

2. The *z*-distribution has a mean of 0, a standard deviation of 1.0, and the shape of the raw score distribution.

3. *z*-scores standardize or equate different distributions so they can be compared and graphed on the same set of axes.

4. a.   It is our model of the perfect normal z-distribution.
   b.   It is used as a model of any normal distribution of raw scores after they have been transformed to z-scores.
   c.   The raw scores should be at least approximately normally distributed, the scores should be from a continuous interval or ratio variable, and the sample should be large.

5. a. $(80-86)/12 = -0.5$
   b. $(98-86)/12 = +1.0$
   c. $(-1.5)(12) + 86 = 68$
   d. $(1.0)(12) + 86 = 98$

6. a. -2.8
   b. $+1.0$
   c. -0.7
   d. -1.9

7. a. -1.7
   b. $+1.0$
   c. -0.7
   d. 0

8. a. $(31-25)/\sqrt{4} = +3.0$
   b. $(18-25)/\sqrt{4} = -3.5$
   c. $(-2.5)(\sqrt{4}) + 25 = 20$
   d. $(0.5)(\sqrt{4}) + 25 = 26$

9. a. $z = -2.3$
   b. $z = -0.6$

10. a. $0.3849 + 0.2257 = 0.6106$
    b. $0.4192 + 0.5000 = 0.9192$
    c. 0.0047
    d. $0.4772 + 0.5000 = 0.9772$

11. a.   In the z-table, you should locate $z = +0.97$; column C is the proportion (relative frequency) of z-scores above $+0.97$. This is the expected relative frequency in each distribution.
    b.   You should compute the $\overline{X}$ and S_X and transform 100 to a z-score in each distribution. Then, in the z-table, you should find each z; column B is the expected relative frequency of scores between the mean and a raw score of 100.

12. a. 0.4192
    b. 0.0314
    c. 0.0037
    d. $0.0082 + 0.0250 = 0.0332$

13. a. $z = (76 - 100)/12 = -2.0$, rel. $f = 0.4772$
    b. $z = (112 - 100)/12 = +1.0$, rel. $f = 0.1587$
    c. $z = (106 - 100)/12 = +0.5$, rel. f below $= 0.1915 + 0.50 = 0.6915$, so about the 69th percentile.
    d. $z = (84 - 100)/12 = -1.33$, rel. f below $= 0.0918$, so about the 9th percentile.

14. a. $(0.4772)(700) = 334.04$
    b. $(0.1587)(700) = 111.09$

15. a. It is an approximately normal distribution, the mean equals the μ of the underlying raw score population, and its standard deviation is the standard error of the mean, $\sigma_{\bar{X}}$.
    b. It reflects all possible random sample means that, using the same N, are drawn from a raw score population having a certain μ and σ_X .

16. a. Because she can't determine the sample's relative standing in this way.
    b. Compute the sample's z-score.
    c. $\sigma_{\bar{X}} = 5/5 = 1.0$; $z = (53 - 50)/1 = +3$.
    d. A z-score of +3 shows that among all random samples of 25 students, yours has one of the highest and least frequent mean self-esteem scores that you could ever obtain.

17. a. Compute the z-score for the sample mean. For the standard error of the mean, $\sigma_{\bar{X}} = 18/\sqrt{50} = 2.55$. Then, $z = (136.42 - 130)/2.55 = +2.52$. From the z-table, scores above this z have a relative frequency of 0.0059; therefore, they occur 0.59% of the time.
    b. By chance, she happened to obtain a sample of rather slow participants.

ANSWERS TO THE TEST

1. c   2. a   3. c   4. b   5. b

Chapter 7
Correlation Coefficients

YOU SHOULD LEARN

1. The logic of correlational research and how it is interpreted.

2. How to read and interpret a scatterplot and a regression line.

3. How to identify the type of a relationship.

4. What is meant by the strength of a relationship.

5. How to interpret a correlation coefficient.

6. When to use the Pearson r and the Spearman r_s.

7. The logic of inferring a population correlation based on a sample correlation.

YOU SHOULD LEARN WHEN, WHY, AND HOW TO USE THESE FORMULAS

1. The computational formula for the Pearson correlation coefficient r is

$$r = \frac{N(\Sigma XY) - (\Sigma X)(\Sigma Y)}{\sqrt{[N(\Sigma X^2) - (\Sigma X)^2][N(\Sigma Y^2) - (\Sigma Y)^2]}}$$

2. The computational formula for the Spearman rank-order correlation coefficient r_s is

$$r_s = 1 - \frac{6(\Sigma D^2)}{N(N^2 - 1)}$$

ONE MORE TIME: A Review

correlational | In a(n) _____ study, there is no independent or dependent variable;

participants' scores are simply measured on two variables. We decide which variable to call X and which to call Y when we ask the question, "Given the

_____ scores, what happens to the _____ scores?" We describe | $X; Y$

the relationship using the phrase "For a _____ X score, what are the Y | given

_____? When a relationship exists, a _____ value of Y tends to | scores; particular

be paired with _____ value of X and a _____ value of Y tends to | one; different

be _____ with a different value of _____. When we use the X | paired; X

variable to predict the Y scores, X is called the _____ variable and Y is | predictor

called the _____ variable. | criterion

Correlational research does not allow us to conclude that we have

discovered a(n) _____ relationship. This is because in a correlational | causal

study, changes in X may cause _____ in Y, changes in _____ | changes; Y

may cause changes in X, or some third _____ may cause changes in | variable

both X and Y.

An important step in examining correlational data is to generate the

_____ that shows the data points from each _____ pair. A | scatterplot; X-Y

scatterplot is a good way to spot data points that lie far away from the other

data points. We call these unusual scores _____. Next, we compute | outliers

the statistic called the _____ _____. A correlation coefficient | correlation coefficient

communicates the _____ and the _____ of the relationship | type; strength

formed by the data.

Types of Relationships

The type of a relationship is the general _____ in which the Y scores | direction

change as the X scores change. When the relationship forms a pattern that

fits a straight line, a _____ relationship exists. In this case, the shape | linear

of the scatterplot is a slanted _____, and it is summarized by a slanted, | ellipse

straight	_____ line. The straight line that best summarizes a relationship by
regression	passing through the center of the data points is called the _____
line	_____.
	If the Y scores tend to increase as the X scores increase, a(n)
positive	_____ linear relationship exists. If, as the X scores increase, the Y
negative	scores tend to decrease, a(n) _____ linear relationship exists. A(n)
positive	_____ correlation coefficient indicates a positive relationship, and a(n)
negative	_____ correlation coefficient indicates a negative relationship.
	If a relationship cannot be summarized by a straight line, then it is
nonlinear; curvilinear	called either a(n) _____ or a(n) _____ relationship. In such
change	relationships, the direction in which the Y scores change will _____ as
	the X scores change.

Strength of the Relationship

consistently	The strength of the relationship refers to how _____ one value of Y
	tends to be associated with only one value of X. The strength of a linear
absolute value	relationship is communicated by the _____ _____ of the
	correlation coefficient. The larger the correlation coefficient, the
greater; consistent	_____ the extent to which the data conform to a perfectly _____
linear	_____ relationship.
	The strongest relationship possible has a correlation coefficient of
±1.0	_____. This indicates that everyone who obtained a particular X score
one	obtained _____ and only one value of Y. Therefore, there is no
variability	_____ in the Y scores at each X, and the scatterplot forms a(n)
straight line	_____ _____. If we know participants' X scores, we can
predict	precisely _____ their Y scores.

A correlation coefficient with an absolute value less than _____ indicates that there is less than a perfectly consistent _____ relationship. As the variability in the Ys at each X becomes relatively larger, the value of the correlation coefficient approaches _____. The closer the coefficient is to 0, the _____ consistently values of Y are associated with only one value of X. Also, as r approaches 0, the _____ accurately we can predict each participant's Y score, the more the scatterplot tends to form a(n) "fat" _____, and the less the Y scores hug the _____ line.

	1.0
	linear
	0
	less
	less
	ellipse
	regression

When the data do not at all conform to a linear relationship, the correlation coefficient equals _____. Then, the values of Y associated with one X are virtually the _____ as those found at any other X. The variability in Y and X equals the _____ spread of the Y scores in the data. In this case, we cannot predict participants' Y scores by knowing their X scores. The scatterplot forms either a(n) _____ or a(n) _____ ellipse, and the regression line is horizontal, thereby indicating no _____ is present.

	0
	same
	overall
	circle; horizontal
	relationship

When collecting scores for a correlation, it is important to avoid the "_____ of _____ problem." This arises when the range of scores on one or both variables is too _____. The correlation coefficient is then _____ than it would be if you had not restricted the range.

	restriction; range
	limited
	smaller

The Pearson Correlation

The Pearson correlation coefficient is used to describe the _____ relationship between two _____ variables, two _____ variables, or one _____ and one _____ variable. The symbol for the

	linear
	interval; ratio
	interval; ratio

r

ΣY; ΣY^2

$(\Sigma Y)^2$

multiply

add

pairs

N

subtract

square root

ordinal

r_s

difference

square

add; pairs

tied

mean

match

+1.0

-1.0

0

Pearson correlation coefficient is _____. In the formula for r, the symbol _____ stands for the sum of the Y scores, _____ stands for the sum of the squared Y scores, and _____ stands for the squared sum of the Y scores. The symbol ΣXY indicates to _____ each X times its corresponding Y and then to _____ the products. N stands for the number of _____ in the sample.

The numerator of the r formula requires that we multiply _____ times ΣXY. From this, we _____ $(\Sigma X)(\Sigma Y)$. In the denominator, the last step is to take the _____ _____.

The Spearman Rank-Order Correlation Coefficient

The Spearman rank-order correlation describes the linear relationship between pairs of scores that each are measured using a(n) _____ scale. The symbol for the Spearman correlation coefficient is _____. In the formula for r_s, ΣD^2 indicates to first find the _____ between the two scores in each pair, then to _____ each difference, and finally to _____ the squared differences. N is the number of _____. Before computing r_s, any _____ ranks must be resolved.

To resolve ties, all participants at a tied rank are given the _____ of the ranks that would have been assigned, had there been no ties. Then, r_s indicates the extent to which rankings on the two variables _____ to form a linear relationship. If all participants receive the same rank on both variables, $r_s =$ _____. If they receive diametrically opposed rankings on the two variables, $r_s =$ _____. If the rankings form no linear pattern of matching, $r_s =$ _____.

NOW DO YOU KNOW?

ΣXY r r_s

correlation coefficient	negative linear relationship
scatterplot	nonlinear relationship
outlier	curvilinear relationship
regression line	strength of relationship
type of relationship	Pearson correlation coefficient
linear relationship	Spearman rank-order correlation coefficient
positive linear relationship	restriction of range

USING WHAT YOU KNOW

1. a. What distinguishes correlational research from experimental research?
   b. What two reasons prohibit drawing causal inferences from correlational research?

2. Indicate when to use each of the following:

   a. r
   b. r_s

3. When is a scatterplot used and why is it used?

4. What is a regression line?

5. What two facts about a linear relationship are conveyed by a correlation coefficient?

6. What is meant by the strength of a linear relationship?

7. a. How does the strength of a relationship between two variables affect one's ability to make predictions about Y when X is known?
   b. Explain your answer.

8. If you have computed the correlation coefficient between two variables to be +1.7, should you think you have observed a very strong relationship? Explain your answer.

9. You correctly compute a correlation coefficient of +1.0 between the variables X and Y.

   a. What does this imply in terms of how the X and Y scores change, the scatterplot, and the degree of linear relationship?
   b. If, instead, you find the correlation coefficient to be 0, what would this mean?
   c. If, instead, you compute the coefficient as –0.45, what would this mean?

10.   For each of the following pairs of variables, what type of linear correlation coefficient should be computed?

    a.   Being first, second, third, etc., at a gymnastics competition and spending the most, secondmost, thirdmost, etc., number of hours practicing.
    b.   Income and IQ score.
    c.   Mathematics aptitude and musical ability, both measured on an interval scale.
    d.   Class rank and scores on a creativity test.
    e.   A person's weight and his or her ideal weight.

11.   When we compute the Spearman correlation coefficient, how do we handle the problem of tied ranks?

12.   A researcher reported an r_s of −0.96 between variable X and variable Y. In terms of the scores, what is the meaning of this correlation?

13.   a.   What produces the restriction of range problem?
    b.   Why is it important to avoid restriction of range?
    c.   How can restriction of range be avoided?

14.   Explain what each of the following correlation coefficients indicates about the direction in which Y scores change as X scores increase, the shape of the scatterplot, the variability of the Y scores at each X, and how closely the Y scores hug the regression line.

    a.   −1.0
    b.   +0.32
    c.   −0.10
    d.   −0.71

15.   What is an outlier?

16.   A study of fitness habits produced the following interval/ratio scores.

Participants	Hours Exercise (X)	Reported Life Satisfaction (Y)
1	2	6
2	0	2
3	5	13
4	6	15
5	1	3
6	2	6
7	4	10
8	4	12
9	3	8
10	4	10

    a.   What is the appropriate correlation coefficient?
    b.   Calculate the appropriate correlation coefficient.
    c.   How would you describe this relationship?

17. a. Generate a scatterplot for the data in problem 16.
     b. Does the scatterplot support your answer for problem 16c? Explain how.

18. For the relationship in problem 16, how confident would you feel about predicting someone's
     life satisfaction given his or her hours of exercise? Explain your answer.

19. Students at Former President High School were ranked according to their grade standing in
     mathematics and in history. Their ranks are given below.

Student	Math Rank (X)	History Rank (Y)
1	4	7
2	6	4
3	5	6
4	10	8
5	8	3
6	7	5
7	3	9
8	9	2
9	1	10
10	2	1

     a. What is the appropriate correlation coefficient?
     b. Calculate the appropriate correlation coefficient.
     c. How would you describe this relationship?

20. Based on the relationship in problem 19, how confident would you feel about predicting a
     student's history rank given his or her math rank?

THE TEST

1. When we find that two variables, X and Y, have a high correlation (say, $r = +0.85$), we know that

    a. variations in X cause variations in Y.
    b. variations in Y cause variations in X.
    c. one or more other variables cause variations in both X and Y.
    d. X may be the cause, Y may be the cause, other variables may be the cause, or some
        combination of these.

2. The Pearson correlational coefficient can be defined as

    a. the appropriate coefficient for correlating the scores from one continuous, interval, or ratio
        variable and one dichotomous variable.
    b. an underestimate of the strength of a relationship due to a restriction of range problem.
    c. determining the average amount of correspondence between the z-scores for the X variable
        and the scores for the Y variable.
    d. the population correlation.

3. With a correlation coefficient, the strength of the relationship is indicated by

    a. the sign of the coefficient, regardless of the numerical value.
    b. both the sign and the numerical value of the coefficient.
    c. the numerical value of the coefficient, regardless of the sign.
    d. neither the sign nor the numerical value of the coefficient.

4. If we plot a scatterplot of X and Y scores and the data points form a very skinny ellipse that angles from lower left to upper right in the graph, we know that the relationship is

    a. strong and positive.
    b. strong and negative.
    c. weak and positive.
    d. weak and negative.

5. The Spearman rank-order correlation coefficient r_s is calculated from

    a. z-scores.
    b. paired rankings.
    c. a dichotomous independent variable.
    d. the products of paired X and Y raw scores.

ANSWERS TO USING WHAT YOU KNOW

1. a. In correlational research, no variables are controlled. Scores are simply measured on two variables.
    b. We do not know which variable changed first, or whether any other variables changed that might be the true cause.

2. a. Use r when both variables are measured using continuous interval or ratio scores.
    b. Use r_s when both variables are measured using ordinal scores.

3. It is used when we compute a correlation, to show the nature of the relationship in the data.

4. The summary line that best fits through the scatterplot.

5. The type of relationship and the strength of the relationship.

6. The extent to which the X and Y scores consistently match to form a perfect linear relationship.

7. a. The stronger the relationship, the greater the accuracy in predicting Y scores.
    b. The stronger the relationship, the more consistently one value of Y, or close to one value of Y, is associated with each value of X, so that knowing X gets us closer to the actual Y.

8. No. Because a correlation coefficient cannot be larger than ± 1.0, you obviously have miscalculated.

9. a. As X scores increase, Y scores increase in a perfectly consistent manner; the scatterplot forms a straight line; and the linear relationship is perfectly consistent.
   b. As X scores increase, there is no consistent pattern of change in Y scores; the scatterplot is circular or horizontally arranged; and a consistent linear relationship does not exist.
   c. As X scores increase, Y scores tend to somewhat consistently decrease; the scatterplot is slanted and somewhat narrow; and a consistent linear relationship exists to a reasonable degree.

10. a. r_s (both ordinal variables).
    b. r (one ration and one interval variable).
    c. r (both interval variables).
    d. r_s (one ordinal and one interval variable).
    e. r (both ratio variables).

11. To each tied rank we assign the mean of those ranks that would have been used had there been no tie.

12. Very consistently, a subject's rank on one variable was diametrically opposed to his or her rank on the other variable.

13. a. A small range of X or Y scores in the sample.
    b. Because it produces an underestimate of the strength of the relationship that exists when the range is not restricted.
    c. By testing participants who exhibit the full range of X and Y scores.

14. a. As X scores increase, Y scores decrease; the scatterplot forms a slanted straight line; there is no variability in Y at each X; and the Y scores fall onto the regression line.
    b. As X scores increase, Y scores increase; the scatterplot forms a slanted, relatively fat ellipse; there is relatively large variability in the Y scores at each X; and the Y scores often are not close to the regression line.
    c. As X scores increase, Y scores decrease; the scatterplot barely forms a slanted ellipse; there is almost as much variability in Y at each X as there is over all Y scores; and the Y scores are not close to the regression line.
    d. As X scores increase, Y scores decrease; the scatterplot forms a slanted, relatively skinny ellipse; there is relatively small variability in the Y scores at each X; and the Y scores are reasonably close to the regression line.

15. An outlier is a data point that does not lie within the general pattern in the scatterplot.

16. a. The Pearson correlation coefficient (r).
    b. $r = 0.99$
    c. As the number of hours exercised increases, the reported life satisfaction scores increase in a nearly perfectly consistent manner. That is, there is a strong positive correlation between these two variables.

17. a.

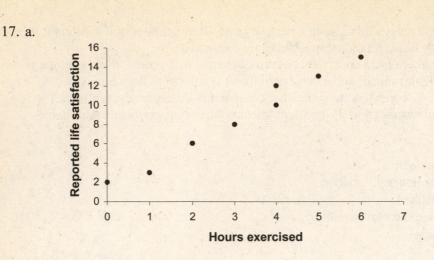

b.   Yes. The scatterplot shows an extremely consistent positive correlation.

18. You should feel very confident because an r 0f 0.99 indicates a nearly perfect relationship.

19. a.   The Spearman rank-order correlation coefficient (r_s).
    b. $r_s = -0.30$
    c.   There is a negative relationship between math ranking and history ranking. As math ranking increases, history ranking tends to decrease.

20. You should not feel very confident about making a prediction because with r_s of $-.30$, the variability in the Ys at each X is relatively large. Therefore, predictions will not be very accurate.

ANSWERS TO THE TEST

    1. d   2. c   3. c   4. a   5. b

Chapter 8
Linear Regression

YOU SHOULD LEARN

1. How a regression line, composed of values of Y', summarizes a scatterplot.

2. How the regression equation is used to predict Y for a given X.

3. How the correlation coefficient implies the accuracy with which Y scores can be predicted.

4. How we measure the errors in prediction when using regression.

5. What the proportion of variance accounted for tells us about the accuracy of predictions when using a relationship to predict Y scores.

YOU SHOULD LEARN WHEN, WHY, AND HOW TO USE THESE FORMULAS

1. The formula for the linear regression equation is

$$Y' = bX + a$$

2. The formula for the slope of the linear regression line is

$$b = \frac{N(\Sigma XY) - (\Sigma X)(\Sigma Y)}{N(\Sigma X^2) - (\Sigma X)^2}$$

3. The formula for the Y intercept of the linear regression line is

$$a = \overline{Y} - (b)(\overline{X})$$

4. The computational formula for the standard error of the estimate is

Variance	Estimated Population Variance
$S_{Y'}^2 = S_Y^2(1 - r^2)$	$S_{Y'} = S_Y\sqrt{1 - r^2}$

5. The proportion of variance in Y scores accounted for by a linear relationship with X equals r^2.

6. The proportion of variance not accounted for equals $1 - r^2$.

ONE MORE TIME: A Review

linear	We summarize a relationship using a procedure called _____
regression; predict	_____ . Linear regression allows us to _____ subjects' Y scores
X	by using their scores on a related _____ variable. The best-fitting
	straight line that summarizes the scatterplot of a linear relationship is called
regression line	the linear _____ _____ . The value of Y that falls on the
Y-prime	regression line at a particular X score is called _____ , which is
Y'; predicted	symbolized as _____ . Each Y' stands for the _____ Y score
	based on the linear relationship with X.
	We read a scatterplot containing a regression line by first choosing a
vertically	value on the X axis. We then move _____ until we reach the
regression; horizontally	_____ line. From there, we travel _____ back to the
Y	_____ axis. In this way, we can tell which predicted Y value is
X	associated with a given value of _____ .
	When we use the X variable to predict scores on the Y variable, X is
predictor; criterion	called the _____ variable and Y is called the _____ variable. We
Y'	can use the linear regression line to determine _____ for any X.

The Linear Regression Equation

Y'; b; X; a	The linear regression equation is _____ = (_____)(_____) + _____. The
slope	symbol b stands for the _____ of the regression line, indicating the
slanted	amount and direction that the regression line is _____ . The symbol
Y intercept	a stands for the _____ , which is the value of Y' when X equals
0	_____ .

Before we compute the regression equation, we compute _____. r

Then, to compute the regression equation, we first compute the _____.   slope

We next compute the _____. The completed regression equation is used Y intercept

to compute the value of _____ at any _____ score. When the data Y'; X

points formed by the X-Y' pairs are plotted, they produce the _____   regression

_____.   line

The formula for computing the slope b looks a lot like the formula for

_____. The numerator for b requires a term where each X value in the r

data set is _____ by its partner Y value and these products are then   multiplied

_____. The formula also requires the values for the sum of X and the sum   summed

of Y, which are symbolized by _____ and _____, respectively. The ΣX; ΣY

denominator for b involves only the _____ variable. We first must X

_____ each X value and then _____ these squared values. We also   square; sum

must add all the X scores and then _____ this total.   square

To calculate the Y intercept (a), we first must have calculated the

_____. We also need to calculate the mean of Y, symbolized by   slope or b

_____, and the mean of X, symbolized by _____. $\overline{Y}$; $\overline{X}$

To find the predicted Y' for participants scoring at any value of X, we

enter the value of _____ into the regression equation. To use the X

regression equation to plot the regression line, we must have at least

_____ data points. To generate an accurate line, we should choose a(n)   two

_____ and a(n) _____ value of X.   high; low

Describing Errors in Prediction

In any prediction, there may be some _____. We first describe the   error

prediction error that occurs when the regression equation is used to

82 CHAPTER 8

sample

unknown

deviates; $(Y - Y')$

squared

variance

$Y; Y'$

$S_{Y'}^2$

least-squares

squared

least; greater

$S_{Y'}^2$

variability

$S_{Y'}^2$; r

square

square root

standard deviation;
standard
error; estimate

average; error

$S_{Y'}$

predict the Y scores in the _____. Using this information, we know about

how much error to expect when predicting _____ scores.

The amount of error in any single prediction is the amount a participant's Y

score _____ from the predicted Y', which in symbols is _____.

We describe the errors in prediction by first computing the sum of the

_____ deviations. Then, by computing the average of the squared

deviations, we obtain a type of _____ that describes the variability of the

_____ scores around their _____ values. The symbol for the

variance of a sample of Y scores around Y' is _____.

The regression procedure we use is called the _____-_____

regression method because the sum of the _____ deviations between Y

and Y' is the _____ possible. Any other method results in _____

prediction error and a larger value of _____.

But there is a considerably easier way to calculate the _____ of the Y

scores around their Y' values. The computational formula uses two terms we've

already learned. These are _____ and _____. We just have to

remember to _____ r.

The most direct way to describe the error in prediction is to find the

_____ _____ of the variance, which produces a type of

_____ _____. This standard deviation is called the _____

_____ of the _____. It is the way we determine the

"_____"amount of _____ when we use Y' to predict Y scores. The

symbol for the standard error of the estimate is _____.

To calculate the standard error of the estimate, we need to take the

_____ _____ of both _____ and _____. These two   square root; S_Y^2; r

values are then _____ together. In order for $S_{Y'}$ to accurately describe   multiplied

the prediction error, we need to be able to assume the Y scores are spread out to

the same degree around all the values of Y'. This is called _____. When   homoscedasticity

data are not homoscedastic, they are _____. In the case of heteroscedastic   heteroscedastic

data, $S_{Y'}$ will provide a(n) _____ description of the average error   inaccurate

throughout the relationship. We also must assume the Y scores at each X form a

_____ _____ around the Y'.   normal distribution

The Strength of the Relationship and Prediction Error

The absolute value of r is _____ related to the size of $S_{Y'}$. This means   inversely

that when r is close to 0, the relationship is _____ and the actual scores   weaker

are more spread out around their associated _____ scores. Because $S_{Y'}$ predicted

and $S_{Y'}^2$ measure the error, they will be _____ when r is smaller.   larger

Conversely, when r is close to +1 or -1, it indicates a _____ relationship   stronger

with _____ error between actual and predicted scores, and _____   less; smaller

$S_{Y'}$ and $S_{Y'}^2$. This tells us that the _____ of a relationship determines the   strength

amount of _____ error.   prediction

The Proportion of Variance Accounted For

We directly compute the amount by which a relationship improves the accuracy

of our predictions by computing the "_____ of _____ _____   proportion; variability
                                                                        accounted
for." The variance we account for when not using the relationship is

symbolized by _____, which is the variance of the Y scores around S_Y^2

_____. The amount by which a relationship permits us to _____ $\overline{Y}$; reduce

Y	this error is the proportion of the variance in variable _____ that is
X	accounted for by the relationship with variable _____. In essence, this
accurate	proportion tells us how much more _____ we are in predicting each
Y'	different Y score when we use the relationship and predict _____ than
$\overline{Y}$	when we do not use the relationship and predict _____.
	The prediction error that occurs when using the relationship is symbolized
$S_{Y'}^2$	by _____. The proportion of the error that remains when using the
$S_{Y'}^2$; S_Y^2	relationship is symbolized as _____ / _____. To find the proportion of total
1	error that is eliminated, we subtract this quantity from _____. This
variance	proportion of total error eliminated is called the proportion of _____
accounted for	_____ _____. The shorter method for computing the proportion of
square	variance accounted for is simply to _____ the computed value of
r; coefficient; determination	_____. This also is called the _____ of _____ The
	proportion of variance in Y that is not accounted for by X is equal to
$1 - r^2$; coefficient; alienation	_____.This also is called the _____ of _____.
	We compute the proportion of variance accounted for in order to measure
important	how _____ a relationship is. Thus, the way to compare two relationships
r^2	is to compute the value of _____ for each. The greater the proportion of
	variance accounted for by a relationship, the more accurately we can be in
scores	predicting _____, and so the closer we are to the scientific goal of
behavior	predicting _____.

NOW DO YOU KNOW?

Y' $\qquad$ b $\qquad$ a $\qquad$ $S_{Y'}^2$ $\qquad$ $S_{Y'}$ $\qquad$ r^2

predicted Y score
linear regression line
predictor variable
criterion variable
linear regression equation
slope
Y intercept
variance of Y around Y'

standard error of the estimate
homoscedasticity
heteroscedasticity
proportion of variance accounted for
coefficient of determination
coefficient of alienation
multiple correlation coefficient
multiple regression equation

USING WHAT YOU KNOW

1. a. What is the linear regression procedure used for?
   b. What is Y'? How is it obtained?

2. a. What is the equation for linear regression?
   b. What does each of these terms mean?

3. What is $S_{Y'}$? What does it measure in terms of

   a. the variability of Y scores?
   b. your errors in predicting Y scores?

4. What is meant by the "least-squares" regression method?

5. a. What is r^2 called?
   b. How is it interpreted in terms of using Y' or the overall Y to predict scores?
   c. Why does r^2 indicate the importance of a relationship?

6. What does homoscedasticity mean? What does heteroscedasticity mean?

7. The following variables are both ratio scores

Participant	X	Y
1	3	2
2	4	5
3	8	9
4	2	1
5	5	3
6	7	8
7	4	5
8	2	2
9	5	4
10	6	5

   a. Calculate the appropriate correlation coefficient.
   b. How would you describe the relationship?
   c. Determine the regression equation.

8. For the data in problem 7,

   a. Find Y' for $X = 2$, $X = 5$, and $X = 7$.
   b. Draw the scatterplot and draw the regression line on this plot.

9. Compute the standard error of the estimate for the data in problem 7.

10. a. If any of your predicted scores in problem 8 are not the actual scores the subjects obtained, by how much do you expect them to be wrong?
   b. How much smaller is this error than if you used the mean of all scores to predict Y scores?
   c. What is your answer in part b called?
   d. Is the relationship in problem 7 an important one? Why or why not?

11. In order to draw accurate conclusions using the standard error of the estimate, what two assumptions must be made about the distribution of Y scores?

12. a. How are the size of r and the size of the standard error of the estimate related?
   b. Explain your answer.

13. Why, as r approaches ± 1.0, does $S_{Y'}$ become smaller relative to S_Y ?

14. Professor Ramirez wants to know if there is a relationship between the number of credit hours in which a student is enrolled and the final quiz score in her class. The scores are given below.

Participant	Hours (X)	Quiz (Y)
1	3	19
2	5	16
3	12	15
4	12	15
5	15	14
6	6	16
7	8	20
8	15	15
9	18	10
10	15	14

a. Calculate the appropriate correlation coefficient.
b. Compute the linear regression equation.

15. For the data in problem 14,

a. calculate the coefficient of determination.
b. calculate the coefficient of alienation.
c. compute the variance of Y scores around Y'.
d. compute the standard deviation of the estimate.

16. For the data in problem 14,

a. predict the Y score for someone who obtains an X score of 6.
b. if the prediction is wrong, by how much do you expect it to be wrong?

17. a. For the data in problem 14, what is the proportion of variance in Y accounted for by X?
b. Is the relationship between these variables valuable? Why or why not?

18. A researcher reports that the multiple correlation between the predictors of height and weight and the criterion of dietary patterns equals +0.68. Explain what this means.

THE TEST

1. The regression line is the line that passes through the approximate _____ of the Y scores corresponding to each X score.

    a. standard deviation
    b. variance
    c. center
    d. range

2. If $r = 0.86$, then the proportion of variance in Y scores accounted for is

    a. $1 - r^2 = .26$
    b. $r^2 = 0.74$
    c. $S_{Y'}^2 = 0.61$
    d. $S_{Y'} = 0.78$

3. Accounting for the variance in Y means that we can

    a. reduce the variability of the Y scores.
    b. identify and predict differences in Y scores.
    c. more accurately use the mean of Y to predict all Y scores.
    d. identify and understand variance in X scores.

4. Which of the following assumptions must be true if $S_{Y'}$ is to be considered an accurate estimate of average prediction error?

    a. The sample of Y scores at each X represents an approximately normal distribution.
    b. The Y scores are all the same value at each X score.
    c. The sample of Y' scores at each X score represents an approximately normal distribution.
    d. The Y scores do not change in a consistent fashion at each X score.

5. The _____ is the statistical measure of how important a relationship is.

    a. variance of Y
    b. correlation coefficient r
    c. standard error of the estimate
    d. proportion of variance accounted for

ANSWERS TO USING WHAT YOU KNOW

1. a. To predict scores on one variable using scores on another, correlated variable.
    b. Y' is the predicted Y score for a participant having a particular X score. We obtain Y' by entering that X score into the regression equation.

2. a. $Y' = bX + a$

b. The symbol b indicates the amount of slope and the direction in which the line is slanted. The symbol a is the value of Y where the line intercepts the Y axis. The X and Y terms represent the scores for each participant on the predictor variable. Y' represents the predicted scores on the criterion variable.

3. $S_{Y'}$ is the standard error of the estimate.

a. It measures the "average" amount the Y scores are spread out around the corresponding Y' scores.

b. It measures the "average" error when predicting Y scores using Y' scores.

4. It is the regression method resulting in the smallest value of $S_{Y'}^2$, and thus $S_{Y'}$, for a given set of data, resulting in the smallest errors in prediction.

5. a. r^2 is called the coefficient of determination or the proportion of variance in Y accounted for by X.

b. r^2 indicates the proportional improvement in accuracy when the relationship is used to predict the Y scores rather than using the overall Y.

c. A goal of behavioral science is to accurately predict scores, and thus predict the behaviors represented by the scores. The value of r^2 indicates how much closer to this goal we come when using a relationship, compared to not using the relationship.

6. Homoscedasticity means that the Y scores are spread out above and below the regression line to the same extent at each value of X. Heteroscedasticity means that the Y scores are not spread out to the same extent at all values of X.

7. a. $\Sigma X = 46; \Sigma Y = 44; \Sigma X^2 = 248; \Sigma Y^2 = 254; \Sigma XY = 245; N = 10; r = +0.91$

b. This is an extremely strong positive relationship.

c. $b = 426/364 = 1.17; a = 4.4 - 5.382 = -0.98; Y' = 1.17X - 0.98$

8. a. For $X = 2, Y' = (1.17)(2) - 0.98 = 1.36$

b. For $X = 5, Y' = (1.17)(5) - 0.98 = 4.87$

c. For $X = 7, Y' = (1.17)(7) - 0.98 = 7.21$

9. $S_Y = 2.06; S_{Y'} = 2.06\sqrt{1 - (0.91)^2} = 0.85$

10. a. You should expect any Y' scores to be in error by an "average" of ± 0.85.

b. Compute $r^2 = (0.91)^2 = 0.83$; the error is 83% less than if you used the mean of all scores to predict Y scores.

c. The proportion of variance in Y scores that is accounted for.

d. Yes. It allows us a considerable degree of accuracy in predicting Y scores, which is a goal of science.

11. We must assume that the Y scores are homoscedastic and normally distributed around Y' at each value of X.

12. a.   As r approaches ± 1.0, the size of $S_{Y'}$ decreases.
     b.   As r increases, the Y scores are closer to the regression line; thus, there is a smaller difference between each Y and Y', and so $S_{Y'}$ is smaller.

13. $S_{Y'}$ measures error using the relationship to predict Y scores; S_Y measures error using the overall $\overline{Y}$. As r increases, the actual Y scores are closer to Y' than they are to $\overline{Y}$, so the error when using the relationship decreases relative to the error when using $\overline{Y}$.

14. a. $\Sigma X = 109;\ \Sigma Y = 154;\ \Sigma X^2 = 1{,}421;\ \Sigma Y^2 = 2{,}440;\ \Sigma XY = 1{,}578;\ N = 10;$

$$r = -\frac{100.60}{126.216} = -0.80$$

     b. $b = -\dfrac{1006.0}{2329.0} = -0.43;\ a = 15.4 + 4.687 = 20.09;\ Y' = -0.43X + 20.09$

15. a. $r^2 = (-0.80)^2 = 0.64$
     b. $1 - r^2 = 1 - 0.64 = 0.36$
     c. $S_{Y'}^2 = \dfrac{68.40}{10} = 6.84$
     d. $S_{Y'} = (2.615)(\sqrt{0.36}) = 1.57$

16. a.   For $X = 6;\ Y' = -0.43(6) + 20.09 = 17.51$
     b.   By an amount equal to $S_{Y'}, or \pm 1.57$

17. a. $r^2 = 0.64$
     b.   Very valuable. Nearly 65% of the variability in Y scores can be predicted or accounted for.

18. When the researcher uses a person's height and weight to predict his or her dietary pattern, the researcher can account for or explain $r^2 = 0.68^2 = 0.46$ of the variance (differences) in dietary patterns.

ANSWERS TO THE TEST

1. c   2. b   3. b   4. a   5. d

Chapter 9
Using Probability To Make Decisions About Data

YOU SHOULD LEARN

1. What probability communicates.

2. How probability is computed based on an event's relative frequency in the population.

3. How the probability of scores is computed using z-scores and the standard normal curve.

4. How the probability of sample means is computed using z-scores and the standard normal curve.

5. How to set up and use a sampling distribution of means to determine whether a sample mean is likely to represent a particular population.

YOU SHOULD LEARN WHEN, WHY, AND HOW TO USE THESE FORMULAS

The formula for transforming a sample mean to a z-score is

$$z = \frac{\overline{X} - \mu}{\sigma_{\overline{X}}} \text{ where}$$

the standard error of the mean, $\sigma_{\overline{X}}$, is found as

$$\sigma_{\overline{X}} = \frac{\sigma_X}{\sqrt{N}}$$

ONE MORE TIME: A Review

The probability of an event is symbolized by the letter _____.	p
Specifically, the probability of a given event (A) is symbolized _____.	$p(A)$
An event's probability is equal to the event's _____ _____ in the	relative frequency
_____. An event's relative frequency in the population is also the	population

expected	event's _____ relative frequency in any sample. Probability is our way of
random	expressing what we expect to occur in any _____ sample; it indicates our
confidence	_____ in any particular random event. We must remember probability is
long run	based on what happens over the _____ _____.
0; 1	A p can never be less than _____ or more than _____. The sum
1	of the probabilities of all events in the population equals _____.

Computing Probability

	When we have computed the probability of every event in a population, we
probability distribution	have created a(n) _____ _____. One way to create a probability
	distribution is to observe the relative frequency of events, creating a(n)
empirical	_____ probability distribution. We do this by examining the relative
samples	frequency of _____ from the population and then assuming these
population	represent the relative frequencies of the event in the _____.
	The other way to create a probability distribution is to create a(n)
theoretical; model	_____ distribution. This is based on a(n) _____ of how we assume
distributes	nature _____ the events. From the model, we determine an event's
population; probability	relative frequency in the _____, which is then the event's _____ in
	any sample.
	When the probability of one event is not influenced by the occurrence of
independent	another event, the two events are _____. When the probability of one
	event is influenced by the occurrence of another event, the two events are
dependent	_____. The sampling technique in which we return previously selected
sampling	items to the population before drawing additional samples is called _____
with replacement	_____ _____. If we do not return previously selected items to the

population before drawing additional samples, we are _____ _____ _____.

sampling without replacement

Obtaining Probability from the Standard Normal Curve

From the z-table, we find the proportion of the total area under the standard normal curve above or below a certain _____. Each proportion is also the _____ _____ of the z-scores in that portion of the curve. Since this is the relative frequency of those z-scores in the _____, the proportion of the area under the curve for certain z-scores equals the _____ of randomly selecting any of those z-scores. The probability of selecting certain z-scores is also the probability of selecting the corresponding _____ _____.

z-score

relative frequency

population

probability

raw scores

We also can use z-scores to determine the probability of randomly selecting certain _____ _____. To compute the z-score for a sample mean, we first compute the _____ _____ of the _____. We use the formula ____ = ____ / ____. Then we compute the sample mean's z-score using the formula $z = ($ ____ $-$ ____ $)/$ ____.

sample means

standard error; mean

$\sigma_{\overline{X}}$; σ; $\sqrt{N}$

$\overline{X}$; μ; $\sigma_{\overline{X}}$

The z-score indicates the location of the sample mean on the _____ distribution of _____. This is a frequency distribution of all _____ sample means that result when a particular _____ _____ population having a particular value of _____ is randomly sampled using the same size _____. The proportion of the area under the normal curve above or below z indicates the _____ _____ of the corresponding means in the population of _____. This relative frequency is the _____ of selecting any of these sample means when sampling the underlying _____ _____ population.

sampling

means; possible

raw score

μ

N

relative frequency

means; probability

raw

score

Random Sampling and Sampling Error

We can never be certain that a sample represents a particular population because

chance   the sample may be different from the population because of _____. If a

sample poorly represents one population, it will appear to represent a(n)

different   _____ population. Thus, we are never sure whether a sample poorly

μ represents one population that has one value of _____ or whether it

accurately   _____ represents another population that has some other μ. When the

scores selected result in a sample statistic that is different from the population

sampling error   parameter it represents, this is called _____ _____.

       To decide whether our sample represents a population with a particular μ,

sampling distribution;   we examine the _____ _____ of _____ that would be created
means
z-score   from that population. We transform the $\overline{X}$ to a(n) _____. The probability

of obtaining this z is the probability of obtaining the sample mean when

raw score   sampling the underlying _____ _____ population. We decide that

close   our sample may represent the underlying population if the $\overline{X}$ is "_____

to" μ. We decide our sample does not represent the population if the $\overline{X}$ is

far   "_____ from" μ. In the latter case, we conclude the sample represents

different; μ a(n) _____ population having some other value of _____.

Setting Up the Sampling Distribution

tails   First, we select the point in the _____ of the sampling distribution where

unbelievable   any sample mean would be _____ and so is unlikely to represent the

population; criterion   _____. This is called our _____. We decide that the sample does

not represent the population when the probability of the sample's occurring in

less   that population is _____ than our criterion probability. We usually use the

0.05   criterion of _____. When the criterion is 0.05, those sample means

falling in the extreme _____ % of the sampling distribution are	5
considered too _____ to accept as representing the underlying	unlikely
_____ _____ population. The extreme portion of a sampling	raw score
distribution containing those sample means considered too unlikely is called the	
_____ of _____. The region of rejection contains the _____	region; rejection; least
frequent, and thus the most _____, sample means we can obtain when	unrepresentative
representing this population.	
The region of rejection begins at the z-score called the _____	critical
_____. If we want to examine sample means that are either above or below	value
μ using a criterion of 0.05, the region of rejection in *each* tail contains the	
extreme _____ of the sampling distribution. The extreme 0.025 of the	0.025
curve lies beyond the critical value of _____. Alternatively, if we are	±1.96
concerned with sample means that are only below μ, the region of rejection	
encompasses _____ % of the area under the curve in the _____ tail	5; lower
of the distribution. This produces a critical value of _____. If we are	−1.645
concerned with sample means that are only above μ, we place the entire region	
of the rejection in the _____ tail of the distribution. Then the critical value	upper
is _____.	+1.645
Our sample mean lies in the region of rejection if its z-score lies	
_____ the critical value. Then either our sample is an extremely	beyond
_____ sample produced by chance when representing the underlying raw	unrepresentative
score population, or it represents a(n) _____ population. Given that	different
sample means in the region of rejection are so _____ to occur when	unlikely
representing this population, it is _____ that our sample represents this	unlikely
population. Therefore, we say that we _____ the idea that our sample	reject

                represents this population. We then conclude the sample represents a(n)

different   _____ population of scores, where such a sample mean is more

likely; unlikely   _____. Thus we are deciding against the _____ probability the

                sample represents the raw score population described by the sampling

likely   distribution and deciding in favor of the more _____ probability the

                sample represents some other population.

                    Conversely, our sample mean is not in the region of rejection if its z-score is

beyond   not _____ the critical value. Then, by our criterion, such z-scores and

likely   corresponding sample means are _____ to occur when representing this

retain   population. Therefore, we say that we _____ the idea that random chance

representative   produced a less than perfectly _____ sample and that our sample may still

represent   _____ this population.

NOW DO YOU KNOW?

p	sampling with replacement
inferential statistics	sampling without replacement
random sampling	representative sample
probability	sampling error
probability distribution	region of rejection
independent events	criterion probability
dependent events	critical value

USING WHAT YOU KNOW

1. a. What is the probability of an event in a sample based on?
   b. What does the probability of an event express?

2. a. What is an empirical probability distribution?
   b. What is a theoretical probability distribution?

3. A student keeps a mood diary for a social psychology experiment. Over a 30-day period, he records that he is happy on 13 days, grumpy on 5 days, sad on 2 days, and anxious on 10 days. Compute the probability that tomorrow he will be (a) happy, (b) sad, (c) anxious, (d) grumpy, (e) in one of these moods.

4. How is the probability of one event affected by whether it is dependent on or independent of another event?

5. Given a standard deck of 52 playing cards, determine the probability of the following events:

   a. Probability of drawing a 7.
   b. Probability of drawing a club.
   c. Probability of drawing a 7 or a 10.
   d. Probability of drawing a 7 or a club.

6. Why is a proportion of the area under the standard normal curve equal to a probability?

7. Find the probability of each of the following:

   a. A z-score below -2.10.
   b. A z-score between ± 0.97.
   c. A z-score below -1.53 or above 2.53.
   d. A z-score below 1.37.

8. It is known that 86% of persons with insomnia also have reported a problem with fatigue. Dr. Delgado's patient Bob reports no problem with fatigue.

   a. Based on this information, should Dr. Delgado decide that Bob has insomnia? Explain your answer.
   b. If further testing reveals that Bob *does* have insomnia, explain how the previous decision in part a of this problem could have occurred.

9. In a sample with a mean of 46 and a standard deviation of 8, what is the probability of randomly selecting each of the following raw scores?

   a. A score above 64
   b. A score between 40 and 50
   c. A score of 48 or below

10. What information is provided by a sampling distribution of means?

11. The population from which the sample in problem 10 was randomly drawn has a mean of 51 and a standard deviation of 14.

   a. What is the probability of obtaining a random sample of 25 scores with a mean of 46 or less?
   b. Out of 1,000 samples, how many would you expect to have a mean of 46 or below?

12. In testing the representativeness of a sample mean,

    a. what is the criterion?
    b. what is the critical value?
    c. what is the region of rejection?

13. a. What decision do we make when we compute a z-score that lies beyond the critical value?
    b. What if the z-score does not lie beyond the critical value?

14. A researcher obtains a sample mean of 66, which produces a z of +1.45. With the critical value of ±1.96, this researcher decides to reject the idea that the sample is representative of the underlying raw score population having a μ of 60.

    a. Draw the sampling distribution and indicate the relative locations of $\overline{X}$, μ, the computed z-score, and the two critical values.
    b. Is the conclusion given correct? Explain your answer.

15. In a study with a sample mean of 14, a z of +2.0 is obtained. With a critical value of ±1.96, the research team decides not to reject the idea that the sample represents a μ of 12.

    a. Draw the sampling distribution and indicate the relative locations of $\overline{X}$, μ, the computed z-score, and the two critical values.
    b. Is the conclusion given correct? Explain your answer.
    c. What population is this sample likely to represent?

16. In problem 14 and problem 15, the sample means do not equal the corresponding μs.

    a. Give two explanations for this occurrence that you might have used before examining z.
    b. If both means differ from their respective μs for the same two possible reasons, why are the final conclusions so different?

17. Consider a population for which $\mu = 53$ and $\sigma_X = 15$. Using a criterion of $p = 0.05$ and both tails of the sampling distribution, which of the following samples ($N = 50$) can be called unrepresentative of the population?

    a. A sample with $\overline{X} = 56$
    b. A sample with $\overline{X} = 47$

18. A test of funniness administered to the population of successful late-night comedians yields a mean of 72 and a standard deviation of 8. Answer the following using a decision criterion of $p = 0.05$ and *only* the lower tail of the sampling distribution:

    a. Is a random sample of 25 comedians scoring $\overline{X} = 69$ unrepresentative of this population?
    b. If it is, what is the μ of the population it probably represents?
    c. What type of comedian would be found in this population?

19. The mean number of hours of television watched per week for the population of all two-year-olds is 20.4 hours. The standard deviation of this population is 4.8 hours. A sample of 40 two-year-olds yields a mean of 21.75 hours of television watched per week. Using a decision criterion of p = 0.05 and the *only* upper tail of the sampling distribution, decide whether this sample is representative of the population where $\mu = 20.4$.

20. The population mean μ on a national scholastic achievement test is 100 with a $\sigma_X = 30$. The students in Mr. Smart's class got the following scores:

127   121   123   128   118   126   120   130   128   119   127   125

Using the criterion of 0.05 in the *upper* tail only, determine if Mr. Smart's class is representative of the population.

21. On a national test of "mental intensity," μ is 20 $(\sigma_X = 6.28)$. Students in your class produce the following scores:

25   26   34   14   33   29   22   18   16   13   21   20   22   21   34   30

Using the criterion of 0.05 and both tails of the sampling distribution, determine if your class is representative of the population.

THE TEST

1. The probability of an event equals

    a. the event's simple frequency in the population.
    b. the event's simple frequency in the sample.
    c. the event's relative frequency in the population.
    d. the event's relative frequency in the sample.

2. The standard normal curve model is a theoretical probability distribution that can be applied to

    a. any normal raw score distribution.
    b. any raw score distribution, whether normal or not, if the distribution has enough cases.
    c. the distribution of any sample taken randomly.
    d. any distribution measured with a nominal or ordinal scale.

3. If a sample is very unlikely to occur when a particular population is sampled, we decide that the sample

    a. was not selected randomly.
    b. was probably one of the unlikely or unrepresentative samples from that population.
    c. does not represent that population and probably represents some other population.
    d. was selected as a result of an error.

4. The edge of the region of rejection closest to the mean of the sampling distribution is at the

   a.   mean.
   b.   critical value.
   c.   0.01 probability point.
   d.   first standard deviation from the mean.

5. The sampling distribution of means describes

   a.   all possible raw scores in the population and their associated probabilities.
   b.   all possible sample means from samples of all possible sizes and their associated probabilities.
   c.   all possible sample Ns and their associated probabilities.
   d.   all possible sample means from samples of one specific size and their associated probabilities.

ANSWERS TO USING WHAT YOU KNOW

1. a.   The relative frequency of the event in the population.
   b.   Our confidence that the event will occur.

2. a.   The probabilities of all possible events in a particular situation based on the observed relative frequencies of the events.
   b.   The probabilities of all possible events in a particular situation based on a model of how the events are distributed in the population.

3. a. $p = 13/30 = 0.433$
   b. $p = 2/30 = 0.067$
   c. $p = 10/30 = 0.333$
   d. $p = 5/30 = 0.167$
   e. $p =$ the sum of all p, or 1.0

4. When dependent, the probability of one event is influenced by the occurrence of the other event; when independent, the probability of one event is not influenced by the occurrence of the other event.

5. a. $p = 4/52 = 0.08$
   b. $p = 13/52 = 0.25$
   c. $p = 4/52 + 4/52 = 0.15$
   d. $p = 4/52 + 13/52 - 1/52 = 0.31$ (because the 7 of clubs was counted twice)

6. A proportion of the area under the normal curve is the relative frequency of corresponding scores in the population. Relative frequency in the population equals probability.

7. a.   0.0179
   b. $0.3340 + 0.3340 = 0.6680$
   c. $0.0630 + 0.00578 = 0.0687$
   d. $0.5000 + 0.4147 = 0.9147$

8. a. Since 86% of those with insomnia report having a problem with fatigue and since Bob does not report having this problem ($p = 0.86$), based on this information the doctor should decide that Bob does not have insomnia.
   b. Although less likely, there is still a probability of $p = 0.14$ that Bob does have insomnia even though he does not report a problem with fatigue. So, although not likely, it is possible.

9. a. $z = (64 - 46)/8 = +2.25; p = 0.0122$
   b. $z = (40 - 46)/8 = -0.75; z = (50 - 46)/8 = +0.50; p = 0.2734 + 0.1915 = 0.4649$
   c. $z = (48 - 46)/8 = +0.25; p = 0.0987 + 0.50 = 0.5987$

10. It provides the relative frequency, and thus the probability, of any range of sample means when all samples have the same N and are randomly selected from a population having a certain μ and σ_X.

11. a. $\sigma_{\overline{X}} = 14\sqrt{25} = 2.80; z = (46 - 51)/2.80 = -1.79; p = 0.0367$
    b. $(0.0367)(1000) = 36.7$ or approximately 37 out of the 1,000 samples.

12. a. The probability used to define a sample as too unlikely to be representative of the population.
    b. The z-score marking the beginning of the region of rejection.
    c. The portion of the sampling distribution containing those sample means defined as too unlikely to be representative of the population.

13. a. We decide the corresponding sample does not represent the underlying raw score population.
    b. We decide the corresponding sample may represent the underlying raw score population.

14. a

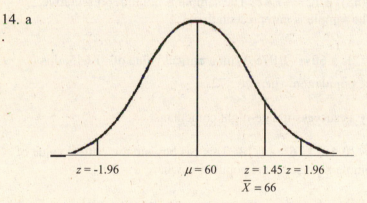

$z = -1.96 \qquad \mu = 60 \qquad z = 1.45 \; z = 1.96$
$\overline{X} = 66$

   b. No, the researcher should not reject the idea that the sample may be representative of the population with $\mu = 60$, because the computed z-score does not lie in the region of rejection.

15. a.

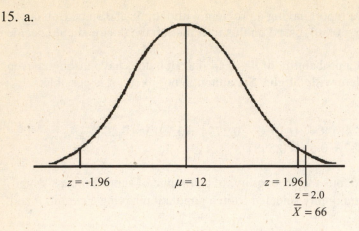

$z = -1.96$ $\mu = 12$ $z = 1.96$

                                                 $z = 2.0$

                                                 $\overline{X} = 66$

b. The team should reject the idea the sample represents the population where $\mu = 12$, because the computed z-score is in the area of rejection.

c. The population where μ is 14.

16. a. Either (1) $\overline{X}$ represents μ but differs from μ by chance, or (2) $\overline{X}$ differs from μ because $\overline{X}$ represents some other population.

b. In problem 14, the difference is likely to be due to chance, and so $\overline{X}$ is likely to represent that μ. In problem 15, the difference is unlikely to be due to chance, and so we decide that $\overline{X}$ represents a different μ.

17. a. $\sigma_{\overline{X}} = 15 / \sqrt{50} = 2.12$; $z = (56 - 53) / 2.12 = +1.42$. The sample is not unrepresentative.

b. $z = (47 - 53) / 2.12 = -2.83$. The sample is unrepresentative.

18. a. $\sigma_{\overline{X}} = 8 / \sqrt{25} = 1.60$, $z = (69 - 72) / 1.60 = -1.875$. With a critical value of -1.645, this sample is unrepresentative of the population where $\mu = 72$.

b. $\mu = 69$.

c. Comedians who are not as funny as successful late-night comedians.

19. $\sigma_{\overline{X}} = 4.8 / \sqrt{40} = 0.76$; $z = (21.75 - 20.4) / 0.76 \doteq +1.78$. This z is beyond the critical value of $+1.645$, so reject the idea that the sample represents the population where $\mu = 20.4$.

20. $\overline{X} = 1,492 / 12 = 124.333$; $\sigma_{\overline{X}} = 30 / \sqrt{N} = 8.660$; $z = (124.333 - 100) / 8.660 = 2.81$

Reject that your class is representative of the population where $\mu = 20$.

ANSWERS TO THE TEST

     1. b   2. a   3. c   4. b   5. d

Chapter 10
Introduction To Hypothesis Testing

YOU SHOULD LEARN

1. Why inferential statistical procedures are used and what they tell us.

2. How sampling error can mislead a researcher.

3. When experimental hypotheses lead to either one-tailed or two-tailed statistical tests.

4. How to set up a sampling distribution of means to test the null hypothesis for one-tailed and two-tailed tests.

5. How to interpret significant and nonsignificant results.

6. How Type I errors, Type II errors, and power affect the decisions and interpretations researchers make.

YOU SHOULD LEARN WHEN, WHY, AND HOW TO USE THESE FORMULAS

1. The computational formula for the z-test is

$$z_{obt} = \frac{\overline{X} - \mu}{\sigma_{\overline{X}}} \quad \text{where}$$

the formula for the standard error of the mean is

$$\sigma_{\overline{X}} = \frac{\sigma_X}{\sqrt{N}}$$

ONE MORE TIME: A Review

When random chance produces a sample containing too many high scores or too many low scores relative to the population, the sample _____ will

$\overline{X}$

μ ; sampling

error

poorly

accurately

inferential statistics

relationship

parametric;
nonparametric
assumptions

normal distribution

interval; ratio

mean

assumptions

nominal

ordinal; skewed

median; mode

experimental

relationship

demonstrate

not equal the population _____, in which case we say that _____

_____ has occurred. Therefore, whenever a sample mean is different

from a particular population μ, it may be because (1) the sample

_____ represents that population of scores because of sampling error

or (2) the sample _____ represents some other population.

　　　To deal with sampling error, we apply the procedures known as

_____ _____. These allow us to decide whether or not we

believe our sample represents a particular_____ in the population.

There are two types of inferential statistics: _____ and _____.

　　　Parametric statistics require certain _____ about the population

represented by our sample data. These include assuming that each population

forms a(n) _____ _____ and that the data are measured using

a(n) _____ scale or a(n) _____scale. It also must be true that the

appropriate measure of central tendency is the _____. Even when the

data do not precisely meet the _____ for parametric procedures, we

usually can employ the parametric approach.

　　　Nonparametric procedures do not require such assumptions. They are

used when the data are measured using a(n) _____ scale or a(n)

_____ scale or when we have a(n) _____ interval or ratio

distribution where the appropriate measure of central tendency is the

_____ or _____.

Setting Up Inferential Procedures

In setting up a study, the first step is to create our _____ hypotheses.

These describe the _____ the experiment either will or will not

_____. If we predict a relationship, but we do not predict whether scores will increase or decrease, we have a(n) _____-tailed test. If we

predict a relationship and also predict the _____ in which scores will

change, we have a(n) _____-tailed test.

The next step is to _____ the experiment. To perform a one-sample

experiment, we must already know the value of _____ under some other

condition of the independent variable than the one we are testing. Then, if we

find the population represented by our sample has a μ _____ from the

known μ, we have demonstrated a(n) _____.

The next step is to write our _____ _____. These describe the

population _____ that our sample mean represents if the _____

relationship exists or does not exist. The statistical hypothesis corresponding to

the experimental hypothesis that the experiment does not work as predicted is

called the _____ hypothesis, symbolized as _____. We write the

two-tailed H_0 for a single-sample experiment by stating that _____ equals

the known value—the value that would be found if the different conditions of

the independent variable represented _____ population of scores. If our

sample mean is different from the μ described in H_0, the null hypothesis

maintains this is because of _____ _____.

The hypothesis describing the population mean the sample data represent if

the predicted relationship exists is called the _____ hypothesis,

symbolized as _____. We write the two-tailed H_a for a single-sample

experiment by stating that _____ does not equal the known value—the

value that would be found if the different conditions of the independent variable

represented _____ population of scores.

two
direction
one
design
μ
different
relationship
statistical hypotheses
μ ; predicted
null; H_0
μ
one
sampling error
alternative
H_a
μ
one

Performing the z-Test

z-test	The _____ is the appropriate parametric procedure for a one-sample
normally	experiment if the population of raw scores is _____ distributed, if
interval; ratio	scores are measured using a(n) _____ scale or a(n) _____ scale,
known	and if the standard deviation of the raw score population is _____. We
null	use the z-test to test our _____ hypothesis. To test H_0, we examine
sampling; means	the _____ distribution of _____ created from the raw score
H_0	population having the μ described by _____. The z-score we compute
z_{obt}	in the z-test is symbolized as _____. In the computational formula for
	the z-test, the value of μ is the value of the raw score population's μ as
H_0; sampling	stated in our _____. It is also the mean of the _____
standard error; mean	distribution. The $\sigma_{\bar{X}}$ is the _____ _____ of the _____.
criterion	To set up the sampling distribution, we first select our _____ for
	deciding whether a sample mean is "too unlikely" to be representative of the
size	H_0 population. The criterion is also the _____ of the region of
α	rejection, for which the symbol is _____. Behavioral scientists usually
0.05	set $\alpha =$ _____. We then arrange the region of rejection in either both
	tails or only one tail of the sampling distribution, depending on our
hypotheses	_____. The z-score that marks the beginning of the region of rejection
critical value	is called the _____ _____. The symbol for the critical value of z
z_{crit}	is _____. When $\alpha = 0.05$ in a two-tailed test, z_{crit} is the value that
2.5	marks the area under the curve that is the extreme _____% of the
± 1.96	distribution in each tail, which gives a z_{crit} of _____.

Interpreting Significant and Nonsignificant Results

If we are to believe that H_0 is true, then our sample mean should be

_____ to occur when samples are drawn from the H_0 population.   likely

However, if our z_{obt} lies beyond z_{crit}, then such a z-score—and our

underlying sample mean—occurs _____, and thus is _____ to   infrequently; unlikely

occur when _____ is true. This is taken as evidence that H_0 is H_0

_____.   false

 Therefore, we say that we _____ H_0 and call our results   reject

_____. By rejecting H_0, we also _____ that our sample   significant; accept

represents a population where μ equals the value described by _____. H_a

Our best estimate of this μ is that it is around the value of _____. $\overline{X}$

 If our _____ does not fall beyond our _____, then we do z_{obt} ; z_{crit}

not _____ H_0. This is because our z and the underlying sample mean   reject

are _____ to occur by chance when sampling the raw score population   likely

described by _____. With such results, we say that we have H_0

_____ to reject H_0 and we call the results _____. We then have   failed; nonsignificant

_____ evidence of the predicted relationship in the population.   insufficient

The One-Tailed Test

In a one-tailed test, we not only hypothesize that our scores will indicate a

difference from the known population mean, we actually hypothesize the

_____ of that difference. In the one-tailed test, z_{crit} marks the extreme   direction

_____% of the curve in one tail.   5

$>$

$\leq$

+1.645; positive

H_0

+1.645; rejection

$<$

$\geq$; −1.645

negative; tail

rejecting; less

H_0

Type

I

large

does

doesn't

α

true

5

0.05

In the one-tailed test, if we predict our condition will result in higher scores, then H_a is written as $H_a : \mu$ _____ the known value of μ. H_0 is written as $H_0 : \mu$ _____ that value. With $\alpha = 0.05$, then $z_{crit} =$ _____. Thus, only a sufficiently large _____ z-score will allow us to reject our _____ hypothesis. Specifically, only a z_{obt} greater than _____ will lie within the region of _____.

If we predict our condition will result in lower scores, then H_a is written as $H_a : \mu$ _____ the known value. H_0 is written as $H_0 : \mu$ _____ that value. With $\alpha = 0.05$, then $z_{crit} =$ _____. This means only a _____ z score in the lower _____ will result in our _____ our null hypothesis. That is, only a z-score _____ than −1.645 will cause us to reject _____.

Errors in Statistical Decision Making

If we reject H_0 when it is actually true, we have made a(n) _____ _____ error. Type I errors occur because the difference between our sample mean and the μ described by H_0 is so _____ we conclude the sample does not reflect sampling error from that population. Making a Type I error is concluding the independent variable _____ works when, in fact, it _____. The theoretical probability of making a Type I error is equal to _____. This is because if $\alpha = 0.05$, we will reject H_0 5% of the time when H_0 is _____. Thus, we expect to commit a Type I error _____% of the time, and so the probability of a Type I error at any time is _____. The assumptions of a statistical procedure are important because if we violate them, then the probability of a Type I error will be

_____ than our α. | greater

    If we need to be very careful not to make a Type I error, we should set

our α equal to _____ . This means our region of rejection is | 0.01

_____ than when $\alpha = .05$. Therefore, the absolute value of our z-score | smaller

must be _____ for us to reject _____. | larger; H_0

    We avoid a Type I error if we _____ _____ _____ | do not reject

H_0 when H_0 is _____. This is concluding that the independent | true

variable _____ work when, actually, it _____ work. The | doesn't; doesn't

probability of avoiding a Type I error equals _____. | $1 - \alpha$

    We have made a Type II error if we do not _____ H_0 when it is | reject

_____. Type II errors occur because the difference between our sample | false

mean and the μ described by H_0 is so _____ that we erroneously | small

conclude the sample reflects sampling error from that population. This

translates into concluding that changing the independent variable

_____ work when, in fact, it _____ work. The symbol for the | doesn't; does

probability of a Type II error is _____. We avoid a Type II error if we | β

_____ H_0 when H_0 is _____. The probability of avoiding a | reject; false

Type II error equals _____. | $1 - \beta$

    Anytime we reject H_0, either we have made a Type _____ error | I

or we have made the correct decision and avoided a Type _____ error. | II

Anytime we do not reject H_0, either we have made a Type _____ error | II

or we have made the correct decision and avoided a Type _____ error. | I

I | Of the two types of error, scientists usually consider a Type _____
 | error to be the more serious.

| The probability a statistical test will reject H_0 when H_0 is false is called
power; $1 - \beta$ | _____, symbolized as _____. As researchers, we want to
reject | maximize $1 - \beta$ so that we are likely to _____ H_0 when H_0 is
false; reject | _____. At the same time, α limits the probability we will _____
true | H_0 when H_0 is _____. Thus, we minimize the probability of making
true | the wrong decision when H_0 is _____ and maximize the probability of
false | making the correct decision when H_0 is _____.

| We maximize power by maximizing the probability our results are
significant | _____. To do this, we select a statistical procedure so as to
obtained; critical | maximize the size of our _____ value relative to the _____
parametric | value. If it is appropriate, we prefer to use _____ statistics, because
nonparametric | they are more powerful than _____ statistics. Moreover, when it is
one | appropriate, a(n) _____-tailed test is more powerful than a(n)
two | _____-tailed test.

NOW DO YOU KNOW?

$<\quad>\quad\leq\quad\geq\quad\neq\quad H_a\quad H_0\quad z_{crit}\quad z_{obt}\quad \alpha\quad 1-\alpha\quad \beta\quad 1-\beta$

inferential statistics	null hypothesis
parametric statistics	z-test
nonparametric statistics	alpha
experimental hypotheses	significant
two-tailed test	nonsignificant
one-tailed test	Type I error
represented	Type II error
statistical hypotheses	beta
alternative hypothesis	power

USING WHAT YOU KNOW

1. a. For what purposes are inferential statistical procedures used?
    b. What are the two major types of inferential statistics?

2. a. What two assumptions must be met by the data in order to perform any parametric procedure?
    b. When are nonparametric procedures used?

3. A researcher obtains a sample mean of 82, although the known population μ is 60.

    a. What are the two possible explanations for why the $\overline{X}$ is different from μ?
    b. What must be done to decide which explanation is correct?

4. In problem 3, the population forms a normal distribution and the data are measured on a ratio scale.

    a. Which type of inferential statistic should be used? Why?
    b. If instead the data were measured on an ordinal scale, what type of statistic should be used? Why?
    c. If the population is only a roughly normal distribution of ratio scores, what type of statistic should be used?

5. a. What do H_0 and H_a describe?
    b. In statistical hypothesis testing, which hypothesis is actually tested?
    c. What question do we answer when testing the hypothesis?

6. a. To which experimental hypothesis does H_0 correspond?
    b. To which experimental hypothesis does H_a correspond?

7. a. What does it mean to predict the direction of a relationship in an experiment?
    b. When do you perform a two-tailed test, and when do you perform a one-tailed test?

8. If we reject H_0, which of the following are true and which are false?

    a. We have proven the independent variable works as predicted.
    b. We have shown H_0 is false.
    c. We have found that a sample of N scores is unlikely to produce a particular $\overline{X}$ if the scores are representing a particular population having a certain μ.
    d. We have proven our sample mean represents a μ around a certain value.
    e. We have proven the independent variable causes scores to change.
    f. We have proven the difference between $\overline{X}$ and μ is not due to sampling error.
    g. We have convincing evidence the predicted relationship exists.
    h. The independent variable may not work, and we may have sampling error in representing this.
    i. We have nonsignificant results.

9. How should each of the false statements in problem 8 be rephrased so as to be true?

10.   If we retain H_0, which of the following are true and which are false?

    a. We have demonstrated the experiment did not work as predicted.
    b. We have proven the independent variable does not cause scores to change as predicted.
    c. We are convinced the independent variable does not work.
    d. We should conclude there is no relationship in the population.
    e. We have no information about the relationship in the population.
    f. The independent variable may work, but we may have sampling error in representing this.
    g. We have significant results.

11.   How should each of the false statements in problem 10 be rephrased so as to be true?

12.   a. What is the statistical definition of a Type I error? Why is it important to avoid Type I errors?
    b. What is the statistical definition of a Type II error? Why is it important to avoid Type II errors?

13.   Andy is conducting a study of whether adolescent males who are enrolled in an anger-management class exhibit more aggressive behaviors than other adolescent boys. For the test of aggression Andy is using, he knows $\mu = 57$ and $\sigma_X = 7$. He collects data on a sample of 25 boys in the anger-management class and obtains $\overline{X} = 60$.

    a. Should Andy do a one-tailed or a two-tailed test? Explain your answer.
    b. State the appropriate H_0 and H_a, given your answer in part a.
    c. Use $\alpha = 0.05$. What is the value of z_{crit}?
    d. Calculate z_{obt}
    e. Using symbols, report your findings.
    f. What should Andy conclude?

14.   In problem 13,

    a. What is the probability the researcher made a Type I error?
    b. What would the Type I error be in terms of the conclusion about the relationship between the independent and dependent variables?
    c. What is the probability the researcher made a Type II error?
    d. What would the Type II error be in terms of the conclusion about the relationship between the independent and dependent variables?

15.   Denise is interested in whether the physical coordination skills among low-income pre-school children are different from those of other children. She knows the population mean for the Pre-School Coordination Activity Test (PCAT) is 120 with $\sigma_X = 10$. She tests 80 pre-schoolers from low-income families and obtains an $\overline{X} = 122$.

    a. Should Denise do a one-tailed or a two-tailed test? Explain your answer.
    b. State the appropriate H_0 and H_a, given your answer in part a.
    c. Use $\alpha = 0.05$. What is the value of z_{crit}?
    d. Calculate z_{obt}
    e. Using symbols, report your findings.
    f. What should Denise conclude?

16. a. What is the meaning of "power"?
     b. To maximize power, what do we ultimately maximize?
     c. Why does this increase power?

17. a. What is the advantage of one-tailed tests over two-tailed tests?
     b. What is the disadvantage?

18. A researcher investigates whether children attending day-care centers have a different degree of emotional attachment to their mothers from those not attending day-care centers. On a national test of emotional attachment, non-day-care children score $\mu = 140$ $(\sigma_X = 12.5)$. For a random sample of 20 day-care children, $\overline{X} = 146.07$ $(S_X = 13.3)$.

     a. What are H_0 and H_a?
     b. What is the value of z_{obt}?
     c. What is the value of z_{crit}?
     d. Report the statistical results in the correct format.
     e. In terms of the relationship between the independent and dependent variables, what do you conclude about this study?
     f. What do you predict as the average score of any child attending a day-care center?
     g. What is the μ for children attending day-care centers?

19. Cherise is working on her master's thesis and is studying whether seniors ages 65 and over take more or fewer prescription drugs when they are treated by a physician specializing in gerontology. From the U.S. Census Bureau, she knows seniors take $\mu = 5$ prescription drugs with $\sigma_X = 3$. She collects data from 20 seniors who are treated by gerontology specialists. The number of prescription drugs each is taking is given below.

4	7	3	0	2	3	5	10	4	6
1	2	0	3	2	4	1	5	2	5

     a. Should Cherise do a one-tailed or a two-tailed test? Explain your answer.
     b. State the appropriate H_0 and H_a, given your answer in part a.
     c. Use $\alpha = 0.05$. What is the value of z_{crit}?
     d. Calculate z_{obt}
     e. Using symbols, report your findings.
     f. What should Cherise conclude?

20. Dr. Sharp wants to know if the students in his college have better than average study skills. He knows that the norms for the Collegiate Study Skills Test report the $\mu = 80$ and $\sigma_X = 8$. He obtains data on a random sample of 15 students from his college. Using the sample data below and $\alpha = 0.05$, complete all the steps for a z-test.

78	84	83	75	79	82	80	79
76	84	80	81	77	79	82	

21.   You hypothesize that children will be more relaxed when they are tested with their mothers present. On a standard test, the national average relaxation score of children tested without their mothers present is 44 ($\sigma_X = 6.32$). You test the relaxation of children when their mothers are present. Using the sample data below, complete all the steps for a z-test.

50	52	68	28	66	59	44	36
32	26	42	40	44	42	68	60

THE TEST

1.   What is it called when chance produces a sample statistic that is not equal to the population parameter it represents?

      a.   A null result
      b.   Sampling error
      c.   Experimenter error
      d.   An alternative result

2.   Under which of the following conditions would it not be possible to use the z-test to test a sample mean?

      a.   The population of raw scores is normally distributed.
      b.   The population contains interval or ratio scores.
      c.   Sampling from the population has been random.
      d.   The population standard deviation is not known.

3.   If z_{obt} does not lie beyond z_{crit} (farther away from the population mean) in the sampling distribution, we should

      a.   retain the null hypothesis.
      b.   reject the null hypothesis.
      c.   not reject the alternative hypothesis.
      d.   conclude our experimental treatment worked.

4.   If you are conducting a two-tailed inferential test to determine whether a set of sample data with $\overline{X} = 24$ and $N = 16$ is representative of a population with $\mu = 29$ and $\sigma_X = 8$, what is the correct conclusion for a z-test using $\alpha = 0.05$?

      a.   Since $z_{obt} > z_{crit}$ (+1.96), reject H_0 and conclude this sample represents a population where μ is not 29.
      b.   Since $z_{obt} < z_{crit}$ (–1.645), reject H_0 and conclude this sample represents a population where μ is not 29.
      c.   Since $z_{obt} < z_{crit}$ (–1.96), reject H_0 and conclude this sample represents a population where μ is not 29.
      d.   Since z_{crit} (–1.645) $< z_{obt}$, do not reject H_0 and conclude this sample represents a population where μ is not 29.

5.   When we say a result is statistically significant, we mean

   a.   a strong relationship was shown.
   b.   an important finding has occurred.
   c.   the results were unlikely to have occurred by chance if the null hypothesis is true.
   d.   we have rejected the alternative hypothesis.

ANSWERS TO USING WHAT YOU KNOW

1.   a.   To decide whether sample data represent a particular relationship in the population.
     b.   Parametric and nonparametric.

2.   a.   The data must be (1) interval or ratio scores that (2) represent approximately normal distributions.
     b.   When the data clearly do not meet the assumptions of the parametric procedures.

3.   a.   Either $\overline{X}$ is different from this μ because of sampling error (the sample is unrepresentative of this population) or $\overline{X}$ represents a different value of μ. That is, the sample represents a different population.
     b.   The appropriate inferential statistical procedure must be performed.

4.   a.   A parametric statistic, because the data meet the assumptions.
     b.   A nonparametric statistic, because the data clearly do not meet the assumptions of a parametric procedure.
     c.   A parametric procedure.

5.   a. H_0 describes the value of μ represented by the sample mean if the predicted relationship does not exist; H_a describes the value of μ represented by the sample mean if the predicted relationship exists.
     b. H_0 is actually tested.
     c.   What is the likelihood of our sample mean if it represents the μ described by H_0?

6.   a.   It corresponds to the hypothesis the study does not demonstrate the predicted relationship.
     b.   It corresponds to the hypothesis the study does demonstrate the predicted relationship.

7.   a.   To predict whether changing the independent variable causes the dependent scores to increase or to decrease.
     b.   You perform a two-tailed test when the direction of the relationship is not predicted; you perform a one-tailed test when the direction of the relationship is predicted.

8.   a.   False; b. false; c. true d. false; e. false; f. false; g. true; h. true; i. false.

9.   a.   We have *evidence* the independent variable works as predicted.
     b.   We have shown H_0 is *unlikely to be true*.
     d.   We have *confidence* our sample mean represents a μ around a certain value.
     e.   We *can argue* the independent variable causes scores to change.
     f.   We have *shown* the difference between X and μ is *not likely to be* due to sampling error.
     i.   We have *significant* results.

10. a.   True; b. false; c. false; d. false; e. true; f. true; g. false.

11. b.   We have *failed to show* the independent variable *may cause* scores to change as predicted.
     c.   We are *unconvinced* the independent variable *does work*.
     d.   We *cannot* conclude there is a *relationship* in the population.
     g.   We have *nonsignificant* results.

12. a.   Rejecting H_0 when H_0 is true. It is claiming evidence for a relationship when the relationship really does not exist, leading to erroneous scientific conclusions.
     b.   Retaining H_0 when H_0 is false. It is claiming no evidence for a relationship when the relationship really does exist, causing us to miss opportunities to learn about nature.

13. a.   Andy should do a one-tailed test because he has predicted the sample $\overline{X}$ will be significantly higher than the population μ.
     b. $H_0 : \mu \le 57 ; H_a : \mu > 57$
     c. $z_{crit} = +1.645$
     d. $\sigma_{\overline{X}} = \dfrac{7}{\sqrt{25}} = 1.40; z = \dfrac{60 - 57}{1.40} = 2.14$
     e. $z = 2.14, p < 0.05$
     f.   The results are significant. Therefore, Andy should conclude adolescent males enrolled in this anger management course exhibit increased aggressive behaviors.

14. a. $p < 0.05$.
     b.   Concluding boys in the population who are enrolled in anger management courses exhibit increased aggressive behaviors when, in fact, they do not.
     c. $p = 0$.
     d.   Concluding boys in the population who are enrolled in anger management courses do not exhibit increased aggressive behaviors when, in fact, they do.

15. a.   Denise should do a two-tailed test because she has predicted that the sample $\overline{X}$ will be significantly "different" from the population μ.
     b. $H_0 : \mu = 120 ; H_a : \mu \ne 120$
     c. $z_{crit} = \pm 1.96$
     d. $\sigma_{\overline{X}} = \dfrac{10}{\sqrt{80}} = 1.12 ; \quad z = \dfrac{122 - 120}{1.12} = 1.78$
     e. $z = 1.78, p > 0.05$
     f.   These results are not significant. There is insufficient evidence children from low-income families have different coordination skills.

16. a. The probability of rejecting a false H_0.
     b. The size of the obtained value relative to the critical value.
     c. It increases the probability we will find significant results, thus increasing the probability we will reject H_0 when H_0 is false.

17. a. One-tailed tests are more powerful, giving us a better chance of rejecting H_0 when H_0 is false.
     b. To reject H_0, we must correctly predict not only the existence of a relationship but also the direction of the relationship.

18. a. $H_0 : \mu = 140; \mu \neq 140$.
     b. $\sigma_X = 12.5; \sigma_{\bar{X}} = \dfrac{12.5}{\sqrt{20}} = 2.80; z_{obt} = \dfrac{(146.07 - 140.00)}{2.80} = +2.17$.
     c. With $\alpha = 0.05$, $z_{crit} = \pm 1.96$.
     d. $z = +2.17$, $p < 0.05$.
     e. The results are significant, providing evidence that changing the amount of day care in the population results in an increase in attachment scores.
     f. 146.07
     g. μ is approximately 146.07.

19. a. She should do a two-tailed test because she is interested in either more or fewer prescriptions.
     b. $H_0 : \mu = 5$; $H_a : \mu \neq 5$
     c. $z_{crit} = \pm 1.96$
     d. $\sigma_{\bar{X}} = \dfrac{3}{\sqrt{20}} = 0.67; z_{obt} = \dfrac{(3.45 - 5)}{0.67} = -2.31$
     e. $z = -2.31$, $p < 0.05$
     f. The results are significant. Therefore, Cherise should conclude that older persons who are treated by gerontologists take a different number of prescription drugs than the population average.

20. A one-tailed test should be used.

$H_0 : \mu \leq 80$; $H_a : \mu > 80$

$\bar{X} = 1,199 / 15 = 79.9; \sigma_{\bar{X}} = \dfrac{8}{\sqrt{15}} = 2.07; z_{obt} = \dfrac{(79.93 - 80)}{2.07} = -0.03$

With $\alpha = 0.05$, $z_{crit} = +1.645$.

$z = -0.03$, $p > 0.05$

The results are not significant. Therefore, Dr. Sharp should conclude there is insufficient evidence to suggest his students have better study skills.

21.   A one-tailed test should be used.
       $H_0 : \mu \leq 44; \mu > 44$.

       $\overline{X} = 757/16 = 47.31; \sigma_{\overline{X}} = \dfrac{6.32}{\sqrt{16}} = 1.58; z_{obt} = \dfrac{(47.31 - 44)}{1.58} = +2.09$.

       With $\alpha = 0.05$, $z_{crit} = +1.645$.
       $z = +2.09$, $p < 0.05$.

       The results are significant. Having the mother present significantly increases a child's relaxation score.

ANSWERS TO THE TEST

       1. b   2. d   3. a   4. c   5. c

Chapter 11
Performing the One-Sample *t*-Test and Testing Correlation Coefficients

YOU SHOULD LEARN

1. The difference between the *z*-test and the *t*-test.

2. How to conceptualize the sampling distributions for *t*, *r*, r_s, and r_{pb}.

3. How to perform hypothesis testing using the *t*-test.

4. What is meant by the confidence interval for μ and how it is computed.

5. How to perform significance testing of *r*, r_s, and r_{pb}.

6. How to maximize the power of *t* and *r*.

YOU SHOULD LEARN WHEN, WHY, AND HOW TO USE THESE FORMULAS

1. The formula for the one-sample *t*-test is

$$t_{obt} = \frac{\overline{X} - \mu}{s_{\overline{X}}} \qquad \text{where } s_{\overline{X}} \text{ is computed as}$$

$$s_{\overline{X}}^2 = \sqrt{\frac{s_X^2}{N}}$$

and s_X is computed as

$$s_X^2 = \frac{\Sigma X^2 - \dfrac{(\Sigma X)^2}{N}}{N - 1}$$

2. Values of t_{crit} are found in the textbook appendices using $df = N - 1$.

3. The computational formula for a confidence interval for a population μ is

$$\left(s_{\overline{X}}\right)\left(-t_{crit}\right) + \overline{X} \le \mu \le \left(s_{\overline{X}}\right)\left(+t_{crit}\right) + \overline{X} \qquad \text{where}$$

t_{crit} is the two-tailed value for $df = N - 1$.

4. For significance testing of a correlation coefficient, compare the obtained correlation coefficient
    to the critical value.

    a. Critical values of r are found in the textbook appendices using $df = N - 2$, where N is the
        number of pairs of scores.
    b. Critical values of r_s are found in the textbook appendices using N, where N is the number of
        pairs.

ONE MORE TIME: A Review

	In testing H_0 of a one-sample experiment, if we know the standard deviation
z-test	of the raw score population, we perform the _____. If we must
t-test	estimate the population standard deviation, we perform the _____. The
random	assumptions of the t-test are that we have a(n) _____ sample of scores,
interval; ratio	that scores are measured using a(n) _____ or a(n) _____ scale,
normally distributed	and that they represent a population that is _____ _____. Our
t_{obt}	obtained value when we perform the t-test is symbolized as _____, and
t_{crit}	the critical value is symbolized as _____.
	H_0 maintains that our sample mean is different from a particular value
sampling error	of μ because of _____ _____. To test H_0, we examine the
sampling; means	_____ distribution of _____. We then compute t_{obt}, which is
z-score	similar to a(n) _____, locating our sample mean on the sampling
	distribution of means that occur when samples represent the population
H_0	described by _____.

Performing the One-Sample t-Test

standard	To compute t_{obt}, we need to compute the estimated _____ deviation.
variance	But first, we'll have to compute the estimated _____. This is
s_X^2 ;standard	symbolized as _____. Next, we compute the estimated _____
error; $s_{\overline{X}}$	_____ of the mean, symbolized as _____. Finally, we compute

_____. The formula for t_{obt} is $t_{obt} = ($_____ $-$ _____$) / $ _____. In the | t_{obt}; $\overline{X}$; μ; $s_{\overline{X}}$

formulas for t_{obt}, the denominator is $s_{\overline{X}}$, which is the square root of (_____ | s_X^2

/ _____). | N

The t-Distribution and Degrees of Freedom

The t-distribution is the distribution of all possible values of _____ | t

computed for random samples having the same _____ that are selected | N

from the raw score population described by _____. The shape of a | H_0

particular t-distribution depends on the _____ of _____ for the | degrees; freedom

samples used to create the sampling distribution. The term "degrees of

freedom" is abbreviated as _____. To have the size of our region of | df

rejection equal to our _____, the appropriate t_{crit} for our study is from | α

the t-distribution having df equal to _____, where N is the number of | $N - 1$

scores in the _____. | sample

   If we predict that the independent variable will simply produce a

difference in scores, then we have a(n) _____-tailed test. In that case, | two

we place _____ of the region of rejection in each tail, and each is | half

marked by the _____ found in the _____. In a one-tailed test, we | t_{crit}; t-tables

predict the _____ of the differences. We then obtain the _____- | direction; one

tailed value of t_{crit} from the t-tables. If we predict that the independent

variable decreases scores, then t_{crit} has a(n) _____ sign, indicating that | negative

the region of rejection is in the _____ tail of the distribution. If we | lower

predict that scores will increase, then the region of rejection is in the

_____ tail of the distribution and t_{crit} has a(n) _____ sign. | upper; positive

   We test the H_0 that the sample represents a population wherein μ

_____ some value. If we do not reject H_0, our sample mean is | equals

likely	_____ to occur when sampling from this population. The larger the
lower	absolute value of t_{obt}, the _____ the probability of obtaining our
true	sample mean if H_0 is _____. If t_{obt} is beyond t_{crit}, the sample mean lies
within; reject	_____ the region of rejection, and so we _____ the idea that our
H_0	sample represents the population described by _____. We call such
significant	results _____, and we accept the idea the sample mean represents a μ
H_a	described by _____. We estimate that our sample represents a
$\overline{X}$	population in which the μ is approximately equal to our _____. If
t_{obt}; t_{crit}	_____ is not beyond _____, we do not reject H_0, our results are
nonsignificant; predicted	_____, and we have insufficient evidence the _____ relationship
population	exists in the _____. When reporting t_{obt}, we must also include our
df	_____.
decreases; increases	The value of t_{crit} _____ as the size of df _____. When the df
	in our sample does not appear in the t-table, we can use the values for the df
above; df	_____ and below our own _____ to estimate the appropriate
critical	_____ value. If t_{obt} falls between the bracketing values of t_{crit} in the
interpolation	table, then we perform the procedure known as linear _____.

Confidence Intervals

relationship	Whenever we obtain a significant result, we describe the _____ that
	we have demonstrated. In the one-sample t-test, this involves describing the
	most likely value of _____, represented by our _____. If we
μ; $\overline{X}$	estimate that μ is equal to $\overline{X}$, we are performing _____ estimation.
point	
	The problem with point estimation is that it is extremely vulnerable to
sampling error	_____ _____.

Therefore, we estimate the population μ by computing a(n) _____	confidence
_____. The confidence interval contains those values of μ that are not	interval
_____ _____ from $\overline{X}$, and so $\overline{X}$ is _____ to represent one	significantly different; likely
of them. In the formula for a confidence interval, t_{crit} is the _____-	two
tailed value at α for $df =$ _____. With $\alpha = 0.05$, we are _____%	$N - 1$; 95
confident that the μ represented by our sample falls _____ the interval.	within
With $\alpha = 0.01$, we have the _____ confidence interval, which spans a	99%
_____ range of values of μ than the 95% confidence interval.	wider

Significance Tests for Correlation Coefficients

In most situations, we want to use our sample correlation coefficient to	
estimate the correlation coefficient that would be found between all pairs of	
_____ and _____ scores in the _____. The correlation	X; Y; population
coefficient for the population is called _____ and is symbolized as	rho
_____. However, before we can be confident of this estimate, we must	ρ
test whether the sample correlation is likely to represent the population in	
which ρ equals _____. The null hypothesis implies that if the sample	zero
correlation does not equal zero, it is because, through _____	sampling
_____, the sample _____ represents the population where the	error; poorly
correlation is _____.	zero
In a two-tailed test, we do not predict the _____ of the correlation.	direction
For the Pearson r, we have H_0: _____ and H_a: _____. In a one-	$\rho = 0$; $\rho \neq 0$
tailed test, we predict that the correlation is only _____ or only	positive
_____. Predicting a positive correlation, we have H_a: _____ and	negative; $\rho > 0$
H_0: _____. The region of rejection is in the _____ tail of the	$\rho \leq 0$; upper
sampling distribution, and r_{crit} is a(n) _____ value. Predicting a	positive

$\rho < 0;\ \rho \geq 0$

lower

negative

ρ_s

sampling distribution

frequency

N; zero

zero

less

zero; critical

value; within

unlikely

zero

reject; accept

zero

sample

I

less; 0.05

reject

zero

negative relationship, we have H_a: _____ and H_0: _____. The region of rejection is in the _____ tail of the sampling distribution, and r_{crit} is a(n) _____ value. For the Spearman correlation coefficient, we formulate and test the hypotheses the same way, symbolizing rho as _____.

We test H_0 by examining the appropriate _____ _____. This is a(n) _____ distribution of all possible sample correlation coefficients that occur by chance when a sample having a particular _____ represents the population where ρ is _____. The mean of the sampling distribution is equal to _____. The larger the absolute size of the sample, the _____ likely it is to occur when the population ρ is _____. If our sample correlation is larger than the _____ _____, then it lies _____ the region of rejection. This indicates that a coefficient such as ours is _____ to represent the population in which ρ is _____.

Therefore, we _____ H_0 and _____ H_a. The sample correlation is significantly different from _____, and we estimate that the value of ρ in the population is equal to the correlation coefficient in the _____. When $\alpha = 0.05$, the probability that the sample actually represents a ρ of 0 (that we have made a Type _____ error) is _____ than _____.

If the obtained coefficient does not lie beyond the critical value, we do not _____ H_0, concluding that the sample may represent a population in which ρ is _____.

Testing the Correlation Coefficients

The Pearson r describes the relationship between scores measured using a(n) _____ scale or a(n) _____ scale. We find the critical value of r	interval; ratio
for α in the _____. The appropriate r_{crit} depends on the value of the	r-tables
_____ for our sample. The df value equals _____, where N is the	df; $N-2$
number of _____ in the sample. When r_{obt} is significant, we describe	pairs
the relationship further by computing the _____ _____ and	regression equation
_____.	r^2
The regression equation allows us to predict subjects' _____	Y
scores by knowing their _____ scores. The size of r^2 indicates the	X
proportion of _____ in the Y variable that is _____ for by the X	variance; accounted
variable in our study. This measures the proportional _____ resulting	improvement
from using the _____ to predict Y scores, as compared to not using the	relationship
relationship.	
The _____ correlation coefficient describes the relationship	Spearman
between two sets of rank-ordered scores. We test the null hypothesis that our	
coefficient actually represents _____ correlation in the population. In	zero
testing r_s, the sampling distribution is composed of the values of r_s that occur	
when _____ equals 0. Critical values of r_s are found in the tables of	ρ_s
_____ using _____, which is the number of _____ in the	r_s; N; pairs
sample. When r_s is significant, we then _____ the coefficient to	square
compute the proportion of variance accounted for in the sample data.	

Maximizing the Power of t and r

The power of a statistical procedure is the probability of not committing a	
Type _____ error. We avoid this error by _____ H_0 when H_0 is	II; rejecting

false	_____, concluding that the data represent a relationship when the
does	relationship _____ exist. To maximize the power of a statistic, we
significant	maximize the probability that the results will be _____.

To maximize the power of the t-test, we select conditions of the

| large | independent variable that are likely to produce a(n) _____ difference |

between $\overline{X}$ and μ, we test participants in a way that minimizes the

variability; N	_____ of the scores, and we maximize the size of _____. All of
larger; t_{crit}	these measures result in a(n) _____ t_{obt} relative to _____, so that
more; significant	our results are _____ likely to be _____.

To maximize the power of a correlation coefficient, we test participants

large	so as to produce a coefficient that is relatively _____. This includes
wide	obtaining a(n) _____ range of scores on each variable, so that we
restriction; range	avoid the _____-of-_____ problem, and thus avoid producing a
small	coefficient that is artificially _____. We also maximize the size of
N	_____. Each of these strategies results in a coefficient that is
large	_____ relative to the critical value, and thus is more likely to be
significant	_____.

NOW DO YOU KNOW?

| $s_{\overline{X}}$ | df | t_{obt} | t_{crit} | r | r_s | ρ | ρ_s |

one-sample t-test   margin of error
estimated standard error of the mean   confidence interval for a single μ
t-distribution   sampling distribution of r
point distribution   sampling distribution of r_s
interval estimation

USING WHAT YOU KNOW

1. What determines whether we use the z-test or the t-test?

2. What are the assumptions of the one-sample t-test?

3. a.   What is the t-distribution?
   b.   How is the shape of the t-distribution affected by df?
   c.   What are the implications of this for selecting t_{crit}?

4. For a research project, suppose you want to compare the mean from a sample of 21 students against a known population mean of 100. You obtain a $\overline{X} = 105$. Although you do not know σ_X, you have calculated $s_X = 20$.

   a.   What are H_0 and H_a?
   b.   What is your t_{obt}?
   c.   What are the appropriate df?
   d.   Using $\alpha = 0.05$ and a two-tailed test, what is t_{crit}?
   e.   Comparing t_{obt} to t_{crit}, what do you conclude?

5. a.   Describe the two ways in which we can estimate the value of μ.
   b.   Which is better, and why?
   c.   What information is provided by the 95% confidence interval?

6. What must we do to a correlation coefficient before interpreting it?

7. a.   How can we maximize the power of a t-test?
   b.   How can we maximize the power of a correlation coefficient?

8. Justin wants to know whether a commonly prescribed prescription drug does improve the attention span of students with attention deficit disorder (ADD). He knows that the mean attention span for students with ADD who are not taking the drug is 2.3 minutes. His sample of 12 students taking the drug yielded a $\overline{X}$ of 3.2. Justin can find no information regarding σ_X, so he has calculated $s_X = 1.4$.

   a.   What are H_0 and H_a?
   b.   What is t_{obt}?
   c.   What are the appropriate df?
   d.   Using $\alpha = 0.05$, what is t_{crit}?

9. A researcher investigates whether daily exercise alters long-term stress levels. On a national survey, the mean stress level of those who do not exercise is 56.35. For a sample of 10 participants who exercised daily for two weeks, the researcher obtained the following stress scores:

40	59	48	36	44	43	45	45	32	37

   a.   What are the conditions of the independent variable? What is the dependent variable?
   b.   What are H_0 and H_a?
   c.   What is the value of t_{obt}?

    d.   With $\alpha = 0.05$, what is the value of t_{crit}?

    e.   Report the statistical results.

    f.   Estimate the value of μ represented by $\overline{X}$.

    g.   Using the preceding statistics, what conclusions should the researcher draw about the relationship between these variables?

10. A researcher investigates whether cigarette smoking by pregnant women results in babies with lower birth weights. In the population, the mean birth weight of children born to nonsmoking women is 116 ounces. In a random sample of 18 babies born to women who smoked heavily throughout their pregnancies, the mean birth weight was 113.6 ounces ($s_X^2 = 8.00$).

    a.   What are the conditions of the independent variable? What is the dependent variable?

    b.   What are H_0 and H_a?

    c.   What is the value of t_{obt}?

    d.   With $\alpha = 0.05$, what is the value of t_{crit}?

    e.   What are the statistical results?

    f.   If appropriate, compute the confidence interval for μ.

    g.   Using the preceding statistics, what conclusions should the researcher draw about the relationship between these variables?

11. A researcher studies whether 15 minutes of meditation each day alters subjects' ability to concentrate. On a psychological test of concentration, $\mu = 17.3$ for nonmeditators. On the same test, the meditators obtained the following scores:

       15   18   22   17   18   18   19   21   19   16   22   20

    a.   What are the conditions of the independent variable? What is the dependent variable?

    b.   Should the researcher use a one- or a two-tailed test? Why?

    c.   What are H_0 and H_a?

    d.   What is the value of t_{obt}?

    e.   With $\alpha = 0.05$, what is t_{crit}?

    f.   In symbols, report the statistical results.

    g.   If appropriate, compute the confidence interval for μ.

    h.   Using the preceding statistics, summarize the conclusions drawn from this study.

12. A scientist predicts that engineers are more creative than physicians. On a standard creativity test, the μ for physicians is 40.5. For a sample of 75 engineers, $\overline{X} = 42.1$ ($s_X = 15.52$) using the same test.

    a.   What are the conditions of the independent variable and what is the dependent variable?

    b.   What are H_0 and H_a?

    c.   What is the value of t_{obt}?

    d.   With $\alpha = 0.05$, what are the statistical results?

    e.   What conclusions can the researcher draw from this study?

13. A researcher investigates whether there is a relationship between family income and frequency of hospital emergency-room visits. He obtains an r of -0.26 for a sample of 62 families.

    a.   What are H_0 and H_a?
    b.   With $\alpha = 0.05$, what are the statistical results?
    c.   What should the researcher conclude about whether this relationship exists in the population?
    d.   To what extent does knowing a family's income improve our accuracy in predicting frequency of family visits to the emergency room?

14. A scientist predicts high school students tend to become less uncertain about their career choice as they progress through the grades. She interviews 30 students and obtains a correlation coefficient between class (ordinal) and career uncertainty (interval) of -0.38.

    a.   Which type of correlation coefficient did she compute?
    b.   What are H_0 and H_a?
    c.   With $\alpha = 0.05$, what is the critical value?
    d.   What should the researcher conclude about her prediction?
    e.   Is the relationship between class and career uncertainty a useful one?

15. A market researcher suspects that taste preferences for different cola beverages can be predicted from their caffeine content. She determines the rank order of eight beverages in terms of taste preference for them and their caffeine content. She computes a correlation coefficient of $+0.69$.

    a.   Which type of correlation coefficient did she compute?
    b.   What are H_0 and H_a?
    c.   With $\alpha = 0.05$, what is the critical value?
    d.   What are the results?
    e.   What should the researcher conclude about the relationship between these two variables?
    f.   How much can the accuracy in predicting taste preference be improved by knowing caffeine content?

16. A researcher computes an r of $+0.59$ for a sample of 8 participants. The researcher asks if there is likely to be a positive relationship in the population.

    a.   What should the researcher conclude about this relationship?
    b.   What is the obvious factor that might produce a low degree of power in this study?
    c.   Why is this a problem for the researcher?

17. The t-test in problem 4 was nonsignificant.

    a.   Give two reasons why this might have been the result.
    b.   List three things that might have improved the power of this test.

THE TEST

1. As the number of cases in your single sample gets larger, the t-distribution becomes

   a. more nonsymmetrical in its shape.
   b. more variable.
   c. closer to the true population mean.
   d. more like a normal curve in its shape.

2. In using the sample mean to make a point estimate of the population μ, you

   a. will be accurate more than half the time.
   b. will be accurate 95 percent of the time.
   c. probably do not obtain a precise estimate.
   d. calculate a range of possible population mean values.

3. In doing an interval estimate of the population μ, you multiply the standard error of the mean by

   a. a one-tailed t_{obt}.
   b. a two-tailed t_{obt}.
   c. a one-tailed t_{crit}.
   d. a two-tailed t_{crit}.

4. When testing a Pearson r, the degrees of freedom equal

   a. N.
   b. $N - 1$.
   c. $N - 2$.
   d. 0.

5. The importance of a relationship obtained in a sample is indicated by

   a. r^2, or the proportion of variance accounted for.
   b. the significance level.
   c. the probability of the outcome by chance.
   d. the ratio of the sample variance divided by the population variance.

ANSWERS TO USING WHAT YOU KNOW

1. We use the z-test when the true standard deviation of the population, σ_X, is known. We use the t-test when it must be estimated based on the sample.

2. We assume that the sample contains interval or ratio scores, that it represents a normal distribution wherein the mean is appropriate, and that the variability of the population is estimated based on the sample.

3. a.   It is a model of the distribution of all possible values of *t* and corresponding sample means when samples have equal *N* and all are randomly selected from one particular raw score population.

   b.   The larger the *df,* the more closely the *t*-distribution approximates the standard normal curve.

   c.   There is a different *t*-distribution with a different t_{crit} for each *df* value.

4. a. H_0: $\mu = 100$; H_a: $\mu \neq 100$.

   b. $s_{\overline{X}} = \dfrac{20}{\sqrt{21}} = 4.36$; $t_{obt} = \dfrac{105 - 100}{4.36} = 1.15$

   c. $df = N - 1 = 22 - 1 = 20$

   d. $t_{crit} = 2.086$ (2-tailed test, $\alpha = 0.05$, $df = 20$).

   e.   Since t_{crit} does not lie within the region of rejection, do not reject H_0.

5. a.   Point estimation—estimating that μ equals $\overline{X}$; interval estimation—creating an interval that contains a range of values, one of which is likely to equal μ.

   b.   Interval estimation, because it takes into account the possibility that $\overline{X}$ suffers from sampling error.

   c.   It provides a low and a high value, and we are 95% confident that the interval contains the μ represented by $\overline{X}$.

6. We must perform hypothesis testing to determine whether the correlation is significantly different from zero.

7. a.   Maximize the difference between $\overline{X}$ and μ, minimize s_{X}^{2}, and maximize *N*.

   b.   Maximize the size of the coefficient, avoid the restriction-of-range problem, and maximize *N*.

8. a. H_0: $\mu \leq 2.3$; H_a: $\mu > 2.3$.

   b. $s_{\overline{X}} = \dfrac{1.4}{\sqrt{12}} = 0.40$; $t_{obt} = \dfrac{3.2 - 2.3}{0.40} = 2.25$

   c. $df = 12 - 1 = 11$

   d. $t_{crit} = 1.796$ (one-tailed test, $\alpha = 0.05$, $df = 11$)

   e.   Since $t_{obt} > t_{crit}$, reject H_0 and accept H_a.

   f. $(0.40)(-2.201) + 3.2 \leq \mu \leq (0.40)(2.201) + 3.2 = 2.32 \leq \mu \leq 4.08$

9. a.   The conditions are presence and absence of exercise. The dependent variable is long-term stress level.

   b. $H_0 : \mu = 56.35$; $H_a : \mu \neq 56.35$

   c. $t_{obt} = \dfrac{42.9 - 56.35}{\sqrt{\dfrac{56.10}{10}}} = \dfrac{-13.45}{2.37} = -5.68$

   d.   For $df = 9$, $t_{crit} = \pm 2.262$.

   e. $t(9) = -5.68, p < 0.05$

   f. $(2.37)(-2.262) + 4.29 \leq \mu \leq (2.37)(+2.262) + 42.9 = 37.54 \leq \mu \leq 48.26$

   g.   The sample mean for exercisers differs significantly from the μ for nonexercisers. Thus there is a relationship in the population such that without exercise, μ of stress scores is 56.35, and with exercise, μ is between 37.54 and 48.26.

10. a. The conditions are smoking and nonsmoking. The dependent variable is birth weight.

   b. $H_0 : \mu \geq 116; H_a : \mu < 116$

   c. $t_{obt} = \dfrac{113.6 - 116}{\sqrt{\dfrac{8}{18}}} = \dfrac{-2.4}{0.667} = -3.60$

   d. For $df = 17$, $t_{crit} = -1.74$.

   e. $t(17) = -3.60, p < 0.05$

   f. $(0.667)(-2.110) + 113.6 \leq \mu \leq (0.667)(+2.110) + 113.6 = 112.19 \leq \mu \leq 115.01$

   g. The sample mean for smokers is significantly less than the μ for nonsmokers. Thus there is a relationship in the population such that for nonsmokers, the μ for birth weights is 116, and for smokers, the μ for birth weights is between 112.19 and 115.01.

11. a. The conditions are presence and absence of meditation. The dependent variable is ability to concentrate.

   b. Two-tailed, because the direction of the relationship is not predicted.

   c. $H_0 : \mu = 17.30; H_a : \mu \neq 17.30$

   d. $\overline{X} = 18.75; s_{\overline{X}} = 0.64; t_{obt} = +2.26$.

   e. For $df = 11$, $t_{crit} = \pm 2.201$

   f. $t(11) = +2.262, p < 0.05$

   g. $17.34 \leq \mu \leq 20.16$

   h. The sample mean of 18.75 for meditation differs significantly from the μ for nonmeditation, and so we are confident of the existence of a relationship in the population: Without meditation, μ of the concentration scores is 17.30; with meditation, μ is between 17.34 and 20.16.

12. a. The conditions are engineer versus physician on the variable of career choice. The dependent variable is creativity.

   b. $H_0 : \mu \leq 40.5; H_a : \mu > 40.5$

   c. $s_{\overline{X}} = 1.79; t_{obt} = +0.89$.

   d. $t(74) = +0.89, p > 0.05$.

   e. The researcher has insufficient evidence of a relationship in the population between choice of these careers and creativity.

13. a. $H_0 : \rho = 0; H_a : \rho \neq 0$

   b. For $df = 60$, $r_{crit} = \pm 0.250$, and so $r(60) = -0.26, p < 0.05$.

   c. r_{obt} is significantly different from zero, and so it is estimated that $\rho = -0.26$.

   d. $r^2 = 0.07$, and so we are 7% more accurate.

14. a. r_S.

   b. $H_0 : \rho_S \geq 0; H_a : \rho_S < 0$

   c. With $df = 30$, $r_{crit} = -0.306$.

   d. Her r_S is significantly less than zero, and so she has evidence to support her prediction.

   e. It is useful to the extent that it accounts for 14% of the variance in career uncertainty.

15. a. r_s.
    b. $H_0 : \rho_s = 0; H_a : \rho_s : \neq 0$
    c.   For $N = 8$, the critical value is ± 0.738.
    d. $r_s(8) = +0.69, p > 0.05$.
    e.   She has insufficient evidence of a relationship.
    f.   Based on this research, we have no reason to believe that there is any improvement.

16. a.   This is a one-tailed test, and with $df = 6$, $r_{crit} = +0.622$. Therefore, the r_{obt} of $+0.59$ is not significant, and so there is insufficient evidence that the relationship exists in the population.
    b.   Because the N of the sample (8) is very small, the study is not powerful.
    c.   Even if the relationship exists in the population, the correlation is not likely to be significant, and his conclusions may be wrong (he may make a Type II error).

17. a.   (1) The sample might accurately represent the population where $\mu = 100$ or (2) you might have committed a Type II error because the power was too low and failed to reject the null hypothesis when it was false.
    b.   (1) You might have selected another condition of the independent variable that would have resulted in a larger difference between μ and $\overline{X}$.
         (2) You might have measured the dependent variable more consistently and obtained a smaller $s_{\overline{X}}$.
         (3) You might have used a larger sample size (N).

ANSWERS TO THE TEST

     1. d   2. c   3. d   4. c   5. a

Chapter 12
The Two-Sample t-Test

YOU SHOULD LEARN

1. The logic of a two-sample experiment.

2. The difference between independent samples and related samples.

3. How to create one- and two-tailed hypotheses for zero difference.

4. How to perform the independent samples and related samples t-tests.

5. How to compute a confidence interval for the difference between two μs and for the μ of difference scores.

6. How r_{pb}^2 is used to describe effect size in the two-sample experiment.

YOU SHOULD LEARN WHEN, WHY, AND HOW TO USE THESE FORMULAS

1. The formulas for the independent samples t-test are

$$t_{obt} = \frac{(\overline{X}_1 - \overline{X}_2) - (\mu_1 - \mu_2)}{s_{\overline{X}_1 - \overline{X}_2}} \qquad \text{where}$$

$$s_X^2 = \frac{\Sigma X^2 - \frac{(\Sigma X)^2}{N}}{N-1}; \; s_{pool}^2 = \frac{(n_1 - 1)s_1^2 + (n_2 - 1)s_2^2}{(n_1 - 1) + (n_2 - 1)}; \; \text{and} \; s_{\overline{X}_1 - \overline{X}_2} = \sqrt{s_{pool}^2 \left(\frac{1}{n_1} + \frac{1}{n_2} \right)}$$

To find t_{crit}, we use $df = (n_1 - 1) + (n_2 - 1)$.

2. The formula for the confidence interval for the difference between two μs is

$$\left(s_{\overline{X}_1 - \overline{X}_2} \right)\left(-t_{crit} \right) + \left(\overline{X}_1 - \overline{X}_2 \right) \le \mu_1 - \mu_2 \le \left(s_{\overline{X}_1 - \overline{X}_2} \right)\left(+t_{crit} \right) + \left(\overline{X}_1 - \overline{X}_2 \right)$$

3. The formulas for the related samples t-test are

$$t_{obt} = \frac{\overline{D} - \mu_D}{s_{\overline{D}}} \qquad \text{where}$$

$$s_D^2 = \frac{\Sigma D^2 - \frac{(\Sigma D)^2}{N}}{N-1} \quad \text{and} \quad s_{\overline{D}} = \sqrt{\frac{s_D^2}{N}}$$

To find t_{crit}, use $df = N - 1$, where N is the number of difference scores.

4. The formula for the confidence interval for μ_D is

$$\left(s_{\overline{D}}\right)\left(-t_{crit}\right) + \overline{D} \le \mu_D \le \left(s_{\overline{D}}\right)\left(+t_{crit}\right) + \overline{D} \qquad \text{where } t_{crit} \text{ is the two-tailed value.}$$

5. The formula for Cohen's *d* for the independent samples *t*-test is

$$d = \frac{\overline{X}_1 - \overline{X}_2}{\sqrt{s_{pool}^2}}$$

6. The formula for computing Cohen's *d* for the related samples *t*-test is

$$d = \frac{\overline{D}}{\sqrt{s_D^2}}$$

7. The formula for computing r_{pb}^2 from t_{obt} is

$$r_{pb}^2 = \frac{\left(t_{obt}\right)^2}{\left(t_{obt}\right)^2 + df}$$

With independent samples, $df = (n_1 - 1) + (n_2 - 1)$. With related samples, $df = N - 1$, where N is the number of difference scores.

ONE MORE TIME: A Review

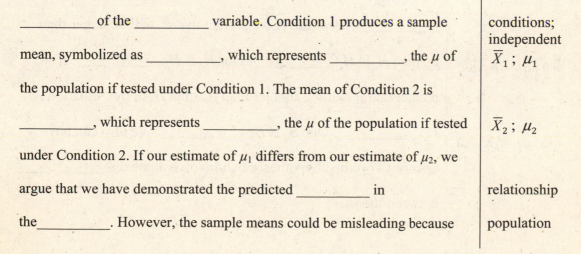

In a two-sample experiment, we measure participants' scores under two

_____ of the _____ variable. Condition 1 produces a sample | conditions; independent

mean, symbolized as _____, which represents _____, the μ of | $\overline{X}_1$; μ_1

the population if tested under Condition 1. The mean of Condition 2 is

_____, which represents _____, the μ of the population if tested | $\overline{X}_2$; μ_2

under Condition 2. If our estimate of μ_1 differs from our estimate of μ_2, we

argue that we have demonstrated the predicted _____ in | relationship

the_____. However, the sample means could be misleading because | population

sampling error	of _____ _____. To test this possibility, we compute _____.
t_{obt}	
	The *t*-test assumes that the scores are measured using a(n)
interval; ratio	_____ scale or a(n) _____ scale and that the populations
normal	represented form approximately _____ distributions that have
variances	equal _____. When populations have equal variances, they
homogeneity	exhibit _____ of variance. When their variances are not equal,
heterogeneity	populations exhibit _____ of variance. There are two versions of
independent; related	the *t*-test, one for _____ samples and one for _____ samples.

The Independent Samples *t*-Test

The independent samples *t*-test is used when the selection of

influenced	participants for one sample is not _____ by the selection of

participants for the other sample. If we predict the two samples

merely represent two different μ values and do not specify the

two	direction of that difference, we have a _____-tailed test.
$\mu_1 - \mu_2 \neq 0$; $\mu_1 - \mu_2 = 0$	We write H_a as H_a: _____. Our H_0 is H_0: _____. If we

predict which mean will represent the larger μ, then we have a(n)

one	_____-tailed test. If we predict that μ_1 will be larger than
$\mu_1 - \mu_2 > 0$; $\mu_1 - \mu_2 \leq 0$	μ_2, then H_a is H_a: _____. Our H_0 is H_0: _____. If we

predict that μ_1 will be smaller than μ_2, then H_a in this situation is

$\mu_1 - \mu_2 < 0$; $\mu_1 - \mu_2 \geq 0$	H_a: _____. Our H_0 is H_0: _____. We also can have

one- or two-tailed hypotheses that involve a nonzero _____

difference	between the μs.

Regardless of the hypotheses, H_0 implies that if the difference between the _____ means does not equal the difference between the _____ means described by H_0, it is because of _____ _____. We test H_0 by examining the _____ distribution of _____ between _____. This shows the frequency of various differences between two sample means when the samples do represent the _____ described by _____. The larger the absolute value of our t_{obt}, the _____ into the tail of this distribution our difference lies, and thus the _____ frequently the difference between our sample means occurs when H_0 is _____.

	sample
	population; sampling
	error; sampling
	differences; means
	populations; H_0
	farther
	less
	true

Computing the Independent Samples t

Computing t_{obt} involves first computing the estimated population _____ for each sample. We produce a weighted average of our two sample variances, resulting in the _____ variance. We weight this average by the _____ for each sample. The pooled variance is symbolized as _____. We then compute the standard _____ of the _____, symbolized as _____. Our t_{obt} indicates how _____ the _____ between our sample means lies from the mean of the H_0 sampling distribution of differences.

	variance
	pooled
	df
	s^2_{pool}
	error; difference; $s_{\bar{X}_1 - \bar{X}_2}$
	far; difference

Interpreting the Independent Samples t

We compare t_{obt} to t_{crit} found for $df = $ _____. When our t_{obt} lies beyond t_{crit}, the difference between our sample means is _____ to occur by chance when it represents the _____ between the population μs described in H_0. We conclude, therefore, the difference between our sample means is _____ different from _____.

	$(n_1 - 1) + (n_2 - 1)$
	unlikely
	difference
	significantly; zero

We accept H_a and conclude that the difference between our sample

predicted

means represents the _____ difference between the two population μs.

relationship;
population

We then have evidence of the _____ in the _____.

Computing the Confidence Interval for the Difference Between Two μs

Our best point estimate of the value of μ that would be found under each

$\overline{X}$

condition is the corresponding _____. Whenever we reject the null

confidence

hypothesis, however, we usually want to construct the _____ interval

difference

for the _____ between the two μs. For confidence intervals, we *always*

two

use the t_{crit} for the _____ -tailed test, regardless of what hypotheses we

have used.

With independent samples, we compute the confidence interval to

μ_1 ; μ_2

describe the difference between _____ and _____. This describes

differences; likely

a range of _____ between two μs, one of which is _____ to be

$\overline{X}_1$; $\overline{X}_2$

represented by the difference between _____ and _____. If $\alpha =$

95%

0.05, we are _____% confident that if we performed the experiment on

conditions; differ

the population, the μs represented by our _____ would _____ by

an amount that falls within that interval.

The Related Samples t-Test

pair

The related samples *t*-test is used when we _____ each score in one

sample with a particular score in the other sample. This occurs either when

match

we _____ each participant in one sample with a participant in the other

repeated measures

sample or when we use a(n) _____ _____ design in which we

measure the same participants in both conditions. To compare the scores in each pair, we first compute a(n) _____ score, symbolized as | difference

_____. | D

Then, we essentially perform the _____-sample *t*-test using | one

the _____ scores. In our statistical hypotheses, the symbol for the | difference

population mean is _____. This is the μ of the population of | μ_D

_____ scores that would result if we measured the population of | difference

_____ scores under each condition and then subtracted the scores | raw

in the two populations.

In a(n) _____-tailed test, we predict the two conditions | two

produce raw scores that merely differ. We then have H_0: _____ | $\mu_D = 0$

and H_a: _____. If we predict which condition represents lower | $\mu_D \neq 0$

scores, we have a(n) _____-tailed test. If we subtract the | one

predicted lower raw scores from the predicted higher raw scores, we

have H_a: _____ and H_0: _____. If we subtract the predicted | $\mu_D > 0$; $\mu_D \leq 0$

higher raw scores from the predicted lower raw scores, we have H_a:

_____ and H_0: _____. | $\mu_D < 0$; $\mu_D \geq 0$

We summarize the difference scores in our sample by computing

the _____, symbolized as _____. We then examine the | mean; $\overline{D}$

_____ distribution of _____. This indicates the frequency | sampling; $\overline{D}$

of the different values of $\overline{D}$ that occur when the mean represents the

_____ described by _____. We locate our _____ on | μ_D ; H_0; $\overline{D}$

this sampling distribution by computing _____. | t_{obt}

Computing the Related Samples t

Computing t_{obt} involves first computing the estimated variance of the

population of _____ scores, symbolized as _____. We then | difference; s_D^2

mean difference	compute the standard error of the _____ _____, symbolized by
$s_{\overline{D}}$	_____.
	Interpreting the Related Samples t
$N-1$	We compare t_{obt} to the value of t_{crit} found for $df =$ _____, where N is
difference	the number of _____ scores. If t_{obt} is significant, we conclude that our
difference	sample of _____ scores represents a population having a μ_D described
H_a; raw	by _____. For $\overline{D}$ to represent such a μ_D, the mean of the _____
μ	scores in each condition must represent the predicted _____.
conditions	Therefore, the means of our _____ differ significantly, and we
relationship; population	have demonstrated the predicted _____ in the _____. Our best
	point estimate of the μ of the raw score population found under each
condition; μ	_____ is the corresponding _____.
	Computing the Confidence Interval for μ_D
μ_D	With related samples, we compute the confidence interval for _____.
$\overline{D}$	This contains values of μ_D, one of which our _____ is likely to
95	represent. If $\alpha = 0.05$, we are _____% confident that if we performed
mean difference	this study on the population, the _____ _____ between the scores
	of the two conditions would fall within the interval.
	Describing the Relationship in a Two-Sample Study
relationship	When t_{obt} is significant, we describe the _____ we have demonstrated.
graph	We first create a(n) _____ of the results. We plot the conditions of the
X; mean	independent variable on the _____ axis and the _____ of the
Y	dependent variable in each condition on the _____ axis. The line

graph is the _____ line we would find for the data and thereby | regression

_____ the relationship. | summarizes

Measuring Effect Size in the Two-Sample Experiment

Following a significant outcome on a two-sample experiment and the

construction of a confidence interval, the next step is to measure the

_____ _____. The effect size tells us the level of _____ | effect size; influence

changing the conditions of the independent variable had on the scores of the

_____ variable. | dependent

One method of measuring effect size is the Cohen's _____. The | *d*

Cohen's *d* measures the effective size as the magnitude of the _____ | difference

between the conditions, relative to the population _____ | standard

_____. According to Cohen, a *d* value of _____ indicates a | deviation; 0.2

small effect size; _____ indicates a medium effect size; and | 0.5

_____ indicates a large effect size. | 0.8

The _____-_____ correlation is symbolized as | point-biserial

_____. In the formula for computing r_{pb} from t_{obt} for independent | r_{pb}

samples, we use *df* = _____; for related samples, we use *df* = | $(n_1 - 1) + (n_2 - 1)$

_____. We compute r_{pb} because _____ indicates the proportion | $N - 1$; r_{pb}^2

of _____ accounted for in the experiment. The proportion of variance | variance

accounted for in an experiment is another way to measure the _____ | effect

_____. The larger the effect size, the more _____ the scores | size; consistently

change as the conditions change, and thus the more _____ the | important

_____ variable is. | independent

differences	Conversely, the smaller the effect size, the greater the _____ in scores
associated	that are not _____ with changes in the independent variable. Therefore,
variables; "cause"	there must be other _____ that also _____ the scores to change, so
independent	that our _____ variable is less important in explaining the variability in
	raw scores.

NOW DO YOU KNOW?

$$N \quad n \quad \mu_1 - \mu_2 \quad \overline{X}_1 - \overline{X}_2 \quad s_{\text{pool}}^2 \quad s_{\overline{X}_1 - \overline{X}_2} \quad s_D^2 \quad \overline{D} \quad s_{\overline{D}} \quad d \quad r_{\text{pb}}^2$$

independent samples t-test
independent samples
homogeneity of variance
sampling distribution of differences
   between the means
pooled variance
standard error of the difference
confidence interval for the difference
   between two μs

related-samples t-test
related samples
matched samples design
repeated measures design
sampling distribution of mean differences
standard error of the mean difference
confidence interval for μ_D
point-biserial correlation coefficient
effect size

USING WHAT YOU KNOW

1. a. What are the two types of two-sample t-tests?
   b. What question are both types used to answer?

2. What is the difference between independent samples and related samples?

3. What are the assumptions of the two-sample t-test?

4. What is meant by *homogeneity of variance*?

5. a. What information does the standard error of the difference provide?
   b. What information does the standard error of the mean difference provide?

6. a. What does the confidence interval for the difference between two population means tell us?
   b. What does the confidence interval for the mean of the population of difference scores tell us?

7. For each of the following, which type of t-test is required?

   a. Studying whether males or females are more prone to simple mathematical errors on a statistics exam.
   b. The study described in part a, but for each male, there is a female with the same reading level.
   c. An investigation of spending habits of teenagers, comparing the amount of money each spends in a video store and in a clothing store.
   d. An investigation of the effects of a new anti-anxiety drug, measuring subjects' anxiety before and again after administration of the drug.
   e. Testing whether males in the U.S. Army are more aggressive than males in the U.S. Marine Corps.

8. Which is more powerful, the related samples design or the independent samples design? Why?

9. a. What does the effect size measure?
   b. How is it computed?

10. A recent study examined the drinking behaviors of underaged college male and female freshmen. Each participant was asked how many alcoholic beverages they consumed during the past 7 days. The researchers wish to determine if there is a difference in the drinking habits of males and females in this age group.

    Sample 1—females: $\overline{X}_1 = 12.9$, $s_1^2 = 3.30$, $n_1 = 13$
    Sample 2—males: $\overline{X}_2 = 11.2$, $s_2^2 = 2.21$, $n_2 = 16$

    a. What are H_0 and H_a?
    b. Compute the appropriate t-test.
    c. With $\alpha = 0.05$, report the statistical results.
    d. What should the researchers conclude?

11. If your results in problem 20 were significant

    a. Compute the 95% confidence interval.
    b. Compute the Cohen's d.
    c. Evaluate the effect size.
    d. Compute the proportion of variability accounted for.

12. On a standard test of attention span in children, a researcher has determined that there is a difference in the population between children who have played board games frequently and those who have not. She wants to know whether the result will be the same when she examines children who play video games extensively. She selects a sample of children who regularly play video games and those who do not and obtains the following attention-span data:

   Sample 1—play video games: $\overline{X}_1 = 12.1$, $s_1^2 = 2.94$, $n_1 = 23$

   Sample 2—do not play video games: $\overline{X}_2 = 11.6$, $s_2^2 = 1.82$, $n_2 = 19$

   a. What are H_0 and H_a?
   b. Compute the appropriate t-test.
   c. With $\alpha = 0.05$, report the statistical results.
   d. What should the researcher conclude about these results?

13. If your results in problem 12 were significant

   a. Compute the 95% confidence interval.
   b. Compute the Cohen's d.
   c. Evaluate the effect size.
   d. Compute the proportion of variability accounted for.

14. Martha believes that a relaxation technique involving visualization will help people with mild insomnia fall asleep faster. She randomly selects a sample of 20 participants from a group of mild insomnia patients and randomly assigns 10 to receive visualization therapy. The other 10 participants receive no treatment. Each participant then is measured to see how long (in minutes) it takes him or her to fall asleep. Her data are below.

No Treatment (X_1)	Treatment (X_2)
22	19
18	17
27	24
20	21
23	27
26	21
27	23
22	18
24	19
22	22

   a. Should she use an independent samples t-test or a related samples t-test? Explain your answer.
   b. What are the independent and dependent variables?
   c. Using the fact that Martha believes the treatment will reduce the amount of time to fall asleep, state the null and alternative hypotheses.
   d. Use $\alpha = 0.05$. What is t_{crit}?
   e. Calculate t_{obt}.
   f. Report the statistical results using the correct format.
   g. What should Martha conclude?

15. a.   Compute a 95% confidence interval on the difference of the means for the experiment in
        problem 14.
   b.   Graph the results of the experiment.
   c.   Compute the effect size using Cohen's *d* and interpret it.

16. Martha believes that a relaxation technique involving visualization will help people with mild
    insomnia fall asleep faster. She randomly selects 10 patients from a group of mild insomnia
    patients and measures how long (in minutes) it takes each one to fall asleep. Each participant is
    then taught the visualization technique and measured again to see how long it takes him or her to
    fall asleep. Her data are below.

Before Treatment (X_1)	After Treatment (X_2)
22	19
18	17
27	24
20	21
23	27
26	21
27	23
22	18
24	19
22	22

   a.   Should she use an independent samples *t*-test or a related samples *t*-test? Explain your
        answer.
   b.   What are the independent and dependent variables?
   c.   Using the fact that Martha believes the treatment will reduce the amount of time to fall
        asleep, state the null and alternative hypotheses.
   d.   Use $\alpha = 0.05$. What is t_{crit}?
   e.   Calculate t_{obt}.
   f.   Report the statistical results using the correct format.
   g.   What should Martha conclude?

17. a.   Compute a 95% confidence interval on the mean of the differences of the experiment in
        problem 16.
   b.   Compute the proportion of variability accounted for using the squared point-biserial
        correlation coefficient..

THE TEST

1. The independent samples *t*-test assumes that the populations from which the two samples are drawn

   a. have equal means.
   b. have equal variances.
   c. have equal numbers of members.
   d. are both skewed in the same direction.

2. The related samples *t*-test is really a(n) _____ carried out on the difference scores for all of the pairs.

   a. independent samples *t*-test
   b. point-biserial correlation
   c. one-sample *t*-test
   d. multiple-samples *t*-test

3. All other things being equal, the _____ is more powerful than the _____.

   a. independent samples *t*-test; related samples *t*-test
   b. related samples *t*-test; independent samples *t*-test
   c. point-biserial correlation; independent samples *t*-test
   d. point-biserial correlation; related samples *t*-test

4. The importance of a relationship is described by

   a. the effect size or proportion of variance accounted for.
   b. the significance level at which the null hypothesis could be rejected.
   c. the size of t_{obt}.
   d. the size of the standard error of the difference between means.

5. A *t*-test is conducted to determine the effectiveness of a new anti-hallucination drug. There are 22 participants in the treatment group and 19 in the no treatment group. Based on this information, which of the following would be correct?

   a. This would be a related samples *t*-test.
   b. The correct *df* for this *t*-test would be $(22 - 1) + (19 - 1) = 39$.
   c. Because there are a different number of participants in each group, heterogeneity will likely be a problem.
   d. This must be conducted as a two-tailed *t*-test.

ANSWERS TO USING WHAT YOU KNOW

1. a. The *t*-test for independent samples and the *t*-test for related samples.
   b. Whether the difference between two sample means represents the predicted difference between two μs.

2. In independent samples, the scores in one sample are not in any way related to the scores in the other sample. In related samples, a score in one sample is paired with a score in the other sample, either because participants are matched on some variable or because the same participants are measured under both conditions (repeated measures).

3. We assume that scores are measured using an interval or a ratio scale and that the raw score populations are normally distributed and have homogeneous variance.

4. Homogeneity of variance means that the raw score populations represented by the samples have equal variance.

5. a. It is the standard deviation of the sampling distribution of all differences between two sample means when the samples represent the populations described by H_0.
   b. It is the standard deviation of the sampling distribution of all means of differences between scores when the sample of differences represents the population of differences described by H_0.

6. a. It contains a range of differences between μs, one of which the difference between our sample means is likely to represent.
   b. It contains a range of values of the μ of differences, one of which our $\overline{D}$ is likely to represent.

7. a. Independent samples
   b. Related samples
   c. Related samples
   d. Related samples
   e. Independent samples

8. The related samples design. Because it reduces the variability of scores, resulting in a smaller standard error, we have a larger t_{obt} that is more likely to be significant when H_0 is false.

9. a. It measures the proportion of variance in the dependent scores accounted for by changing the conditions of the independent variable in the experiment, thus indicating how consistently close to the mean of each condition the scores lie.
   b. By computing the squared r_{pb}.

10. a. $H_0 : \mu_1 - \mu_2 = 0; H_a : \mu_1 - \mu_2 \neq 0$
    b. $t_{obt} = \dfrac{12.9 - 11.2}{\sqrt{\left[\dfrac{(12)(3.30) + (15)(2.21)}{27}\right][0.077 + 0.063]}} = \dfrac{1.7}{\sqrt{[2.694][0.140]}} = 2.77$
    c. $t(27) = 2.77, p < 0.05$
    d. That there is a significant difference between the drinking habits of male and female college freshmen.

11. a. $0.44 \leq \mu_1 - \mu_2 \leq 2.96$
    b. $d = \dfrac{12.9 - 11.2}{\sqrt{\left[\dfrac{(12)(3.30) + (15)(2.21)}{27}\right]}} = \dfrac{1.7}{1.64} = 1.04$

c.   This is a large effect size.

d. $r_{pg}^2 = \dfrac{2.77^2}{2.77^2 + 27} = 0.22$

12. a. $H_0 : \mu_1 - \mu_2 = 0; H_a : \mu_1 - \mu_2 \neq 0$

b. $s_{\bar{X}_1 - \bar{X}_2} = 0.48, t_{obt} = [(12.10 - 11.60) - 0]/0.48 = -1.04.$

c.   With $df = 40$, $t_{crit} = \pm 2.021$, and so $t(40) = -1.04, p > 0.05.$

d.   The difference between means of 0.5 is not significant. Therefore, we have insufficient evidence that a difference exists in attention span scores between children who play video games and those who do not is not.

13. The results of problem 12 are not significant. Therefore, a confidence interval and effect size should not be calculated.

14. a.   She should use an independent samples t-test. Participants were not matched and repeated measures were not taken.

b.   The independent variable is mild insomnia treatment condition (use of visualization therapy versus no use of the therapy). The dependent variable is length of time (in minutes) it took to fall asleep.

c. $H_0 : \mu_1 - \mu_2 \leq 0; H_a : \mu_1 - \mu_2 > 0$ [Because those who did not receive the treatment would have higher scores than those who did receive the treatment.]

d. $t_{crit} = 1.734$ [One-tailed test, $df = 18$]

e. $t_{obt} = \dfrac{23.10 - 21.1}{\sqrt{\left[\dfrac{(9)(8.767) + (9)(9.211)}{9 + 9}\right]\left[\dfrac{1}{10} + \dfrac{1}{10}\right]}} = 1.49$

f. $t(18) = 1.49, p > 0.05$

g.   Based on the results of the independent samples t-test, Martha should conclude there is insufficient evidence that the treatment is effective.

15. a.   Because the t-test is not significant, a confidence interval should not be computed.

b.

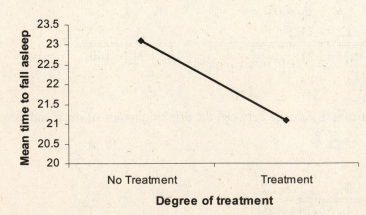

Mean time to fall asleep as a function of degree of treatment

c.   Again, because the t-test is not significant, the effect size should not be computed.

16. a.   She should use a related samples *t*-test because participants were measured before and after treatment (repeated measures).

    b.   The independent variable is mild insomnia treatment condition (use of the visualization therapy versus no use of the therapy). The dependent variable is length of time (in minutes) it took to fall asleep).

    c. $H_0 : \mu_D \leq 0; H_a : \mu_D > 0$ [Where D = no treatment – treatment, because the scores are predicted to be lower after the treatment than before the treatment.]

    d. $t_{crit} = 1.833$ [One-tailed test, $df = 9$]

    e. $t_{obt} = \dfrac{2}{\sqrt{\dfrac{118 - \dfrac{20^2}{10}}{\dfrac{9}{10}}}} = \dfrac{2}{\sqrt{0.867}} = 2.15$

    f. $t(9) = 2.15, p < 0.05$

    g.   Based on the related samples *t*-test, Martha should conclude that the therapy is effective in decreasing the amount of time it takes these individuals to fall asleep.

17. a. $-0.11 \leq \mu_D \leq 4.11$

    b. $r_{pb}^2 = 0.34$, indicating that changing from no treatment to treatment accounts for 34% of the variance in time to fall asleep.

ANSWERS TO THE TEST

    1. b   2. c   3. b   4. a   5. b

Chapter 13
The One-Way Analysis of Variance

YOU SHOULD LEARN

1. The terminology of analysis of variance.

2. Why we compute F_{obt}, and why post hoc tests are needed.

3. What is meant by treatment variance and error variance.

4. Why F_{obt} should equal 1 if H_0 is true and why F_{obt} is greater than 1 if H_0 is false.

5. How to compute F_{obt}, Fisher's protected t-test, and Tukey's HSD.

6. How eta squared describes the effect size of the independent variable.

YOU SHOULD LEARN WHEN, WHY, AND HOW TO USE THESE FORMULAS

1. The formula for SS_{tot} is

$$SS_{tot} = \Sigma X_{tot}^2 - \left(\frac{(\Sigma X_{tot})^2}{N} \right)$$

2. The formula for SS_{bn} is

$$SS_{bn} = \Sigma \left(\frac{(\text{Sum of scores in the column})^2}{n \text{ of scores in the column}} \right) - \left(\frac{(\Sigma X_{tot})^2}{N} \right)$$

3. The formula for SS_{wn} is

$$SS_{wn} = SS_{tot} - SS_{bn}$$

4. The formula for MS_{bn} is

$$MS_{bn} = \frac{SS_{bn}}{df_{bn}}, \qquad \text{with } df_{bn} = k - 1, \text{where } k \text{ is the number of levels in the factor.}$$

5. The formula for MS_{wn} is

$$MS_{wn} = \frac{SS_{wn}}{df_{wn}} \qquad \text{with } df_{wn} = N - k, \text{ where } N \text{ is the total } N \text{ of the study.}$$

6. The formula for the F_{obt} is

$$F_{obt} = \frac{MS_{bn}}{MS_{wn}}$$

Critical values of F are found in the textbook appendices (Table C.5).

7. The formula for the Fisher's protected t-test is

$$t_{obt} = \frac{\overline{X}_1 - \overline{X}_2}{\sqrt{MS_{wn}\left(\frac{1}{n_1} + \frac{1}{n_2}\right)}}$$

The value of t_{crit} is the two-tailed value for df_{wn}.

8. The formula for the HSD is

$$HSD = (q_k)\left(\sqrt{\frac{MS_{wn}}{n}}\right)$$

Values of q_k are found in the textbook appendices (Table C.6).

9. The formula for the confidence interval for a single μ is

$$\left(\frac{\sqrt{MS_{wn}}}{n}\right)(-t_{crit}) + \overline{X} \le \mu \le \left(\frac{\sqrt{MS_{wn}}}{n}\right)(+t_{crit}) + \overline{X}$$

The value of t_{crit} is the two-tailed value for df_{wn}.

10. The formula for eta squared is

$$\eta^2 = \frac{SS_{bn}}{SS_{tot}}$$

ONE MORE TIME: A Review

The parametric procedure for significance testing in an experiment in which

analysis of

there are two or more sample means is called _____ _____

variance; ANOVA

_____, which is shortened to _____. The ANOVA assumes that

interval

the dependent variable measures a(n) _____ scale or a(n)

ratio; normally
distributed
homogenous

_____ scale that is _____ _____ . It also assumes

_____ variances.

factor

An independent variable is also called a(n) _____. When the

one-way

experiment involves only one factor, a(n) _____ - _____

ANOVA is performed. If the participants in the different conditions of the

between

independent variable form independent samples, we have a(n) _____ -

subjects

_____ factor. When the conditions of the independent variable form

within-subjects

related samples, we have a(n) _____ - _____ factor. Each

level

condition of an independent variable is called a(n) _____. Levels also

treatments

are called _____. The number of levels or treatments in a factor is

k

symbolized as _____.

μ

The mean of each level represents the _____ that would occur if

we tested the population under that level. If we can infer different values of

relationship

μ for the different levels, we have demonstrated a(n) _____ in the

population

_____. However, differences in the sample means may be misleading

sampling error

us because of _____ _____. Therefore, we must perform

hypothesis

_____ testing.

When there are only two levels of the independent variable, we can

t-test; ANOVA

perform either the _____ or _____. However, when there are

t-tests

more than two levels, we cannot test all pairs of means using _____.

This is because such t-tests influence Type _____ errors. That is, — **I**

rejecting H_0 when H_0 is _____. The probability of making a Type I — **true**

error in at least one comparison of two means in an experiment is called the

_____ error rate. When there are two levels, the experimentwise error — **experimentwise**

rate using a t-test equals our _____. When there are more than two — α

levels, the experimentwise error rate using t-tests is _____ than our — **greater**

α. Therefore, with more than two levels, we must perform a(n) _____ — **ANOVA**

so the experimentwise error rate equals _____. — α

ANOVA tests only _____-tailed hypotheses. H_0 maintains that — **two**

all μs represented by the sample means are _____. H_a maintains that — **equal**

_____ or more μs are _____. The statistic we compute is — **two; different**

_____, which we compare to _____. If F_{obt} is significant, it — F_{obt}; F_{crit}

indicates that somewhere among the levels there are at least _____ — **two**

means that are _____ different. When F_{obt} is significant and k is at — **significantly**

least _____, we must also perform _____ _____ — **3; post hoc**

comparisons. These allow us to test the difference between every

_____ of means. We can then identify which specific _____ — **pair; levels**

represent different _____. — μs

Understanding the ANOVA

In ANOVA, we compute _____ variance components. These are — **two**

called the _____ square _____ groups and the mean square — **mean; within**

_____ groups. The mean square within groups is symbolized as — **between**

_____. It measures the _____ of the scores within each — MS_{wn}; **variability**

_____ of the independent variable. Because the MS_{wn} is not influenced — **condition**

independent	by the _____ variable, its value does not change based on whether H_0
true	is _____ or false.
mean; between	The _____ square _____ groups is symbolized as
MS_{bn}; means	_____. It compares the _____ of the different treatment
levels	_____. If H_0 is true, the differences between these means is due to
sampling error	_____ _____. Also, if H_0 is true, our scores are from only
one; equal	_____ population. This means that MS_{bn} will _____ MS_{wn}.
MS_{bn}; MS_{wn}	We compute F_{obt} as the ratio of _____/_____. If H_0 is true, MS_{bn} and
equal; 1	MS_{wn} should be _____, and so F_{obt} should equal _____.
	However, if the data are not perfectly representative, then MS_{bn} may be
greater; greater	_____ than MS_{wn}, and F_{obt} may be _____ than 1 because of
sampling error	_____ _____. On the other hand, if H_a is true, this also means
greater; larger	MS_{bn} will be _____ than MS_{wn}, and so F_{obt} will be _____ than
	1. When F_{obt} becomes so large sampling error won't explain it, we
reject; H_a	_____ H_0 and accept _____.
variance; population	MS_{wn} estimates the _____ of scores in the _____, which we
error	call the _____ variance. When H_0 is true, MS_{bn} also represents the
error variance	_____ _____. When H_0 is false and H_a is true, MS_{bn} represents
error; treatment	both _____ variance and _____ variance.

Performing the ANOVA

MS_{bn}	To compute the F-ratio, we must have already computed _____ and
MS_{wn}	_____. To compute each mean square, we must have computed the
sum; squares; df	appropriate _____ of _____ and the appropriate _____.
SS_{tot}	We first compute the total sum of squares, symbolized as _____. We

then compute the sum of squares between groups, symbolized as

_____. We also compute the sum of squares within groups, | SS_{bn}

symbolized as _____. | SS_{wn}

Similarly, the symbol for df between groups is _____. The | df_{bn}

degrees of freedom between groups equals _____ where k is the | $k - 1$

number of _____ in the independent variable. The symbol for | levels

df within groups is _____. The symbol for total df is _____ | df_{wn}; df_{tot}

and is equal to _____. The degrees of freedom within groups equals | $N - 1$

_____ where N is the _____ N in the study. | $N - k$; total

Next, we compute the _____ _____. For MS_{bn}, we divide | mean squares

_____ by _____. For MS_{wn}, we divide _____ by | SS_{bn}; df_{bn}; SS_{wn}

_____. Finally, by dividing _____ by _____, we compute | df_{wn}; MS_{bn}; MS_{wn}

_____. To help us keep track of these components we create a | F_{obt}

_____ _____. | summary table

Interpreting F

We obtain F_{crit} from the F-tables using _____ and _____. The | df_{bn}; df_{wn}

degrees of freedom help us identify exactly which F-distribution we need to

find our _____. This is because there are really _____ different | F_{crit}; many

F-distributions, each with a slightly different _____. All F- | shape

distributions, however, are _____. | skewed

If our F_{obt} is larger than F_{crit}, then we _____ H_0, and F_{obt} is | reject

_____. This indicates the differences between our sample means are | significant

_____ to occur if all means represent one _____. Therefore, we | unlikely; μ

accept H_a, concluding that at least _____ of our sample means differ | two

μs

relationship;
population

reject

relationship

significantly, representing different population _____, and thus

representing a(n) _____ in the _____.

If F_{obt} is not larger than F_{crit}, we cannot _____ H_0, we have

insufficient evidence of a(n) _____ in the population.

Post Hoc Comparisons

We perform post hoc comparisons whenever we compute a(n)

significant; levels

Fisher's

t-test

independent; pair

_____ F_{obt}. Then, we determine which _____ differ

significantly. If the *n*s in all levels are *not* equal, we perform the _____

protected _____. This is analogous to performing the *t*-test for two

_____ samples on every possible _____ of means.

If the *n*s in all levels of the factor are equal, we can compute either the

Fisher's protected;
Tukey's *HSD*
difference

_____ _____ *t*-test or the _____ _____. We

compute the value of *HSD* and then determine the _____ between each

pair of means. Two means differ significantly if the difference between them

greater

is _____ than the value of *HSD*.

Additional Procedures in the One-Way ANOVA

relationship

When F_{obt} is significant, we must further describe the _____ we have

demonstrated. First, we describe the population μ represented by the mean of

confidence interval

two-tailed

df_{wn}

graph

Y

any level by computing the _____ _____. To compute the

confidence interval, we must use the _____-_____ t_{crit} value. We

also use _____ as our degrees of freedom.

It is also desirable to create a(n) _____ of the results. We place

the dependent variable on the _____ axis and the levels of the factor on the _____ axis. Then we plot the _____ of each level. We graph _____ means for the levels of the independent variable.

    We also should determine how much impact the independent variable has had on the dependent variable. scores. This is called the _____ _____. To do this, we compute the statistic called _____ _____, symbolized as _____. Eta is a new _____ _____.

    By squaring eta, we compute the proportion of _____ _____ _____. This is the proportion of variance in the _____ variable accounted for by changing the _____ of the _____ variable. The larger the η^2, the more _____ the effect of changing the levels of the factor, and thus the _____ important the factor in explaining the differences in scores.

X; mean
all
effect
size; eta
squared; η^2; correlation coefficient
variance
accounted for
dependent; conditions
independent; consistent
more

Statistics in Published Research: Reporting ANOVA

When we report our findings from an ANOVA, we should include not only the value for _____, but also the df_{bn} and _____. We should indicate which _____ _____ test we used, as well as our _____ level. From our post hoc results, we should state which _____ or levels were significantly different. We probably should also state our _____ _____ as measured by η^2 and our _____ interval.

F_{obt}; df_{wn}
post hoc
α
means
effect size; confidence

NOW DO YOU KNOW?

$k \quad SS_{tot} \quad SS_{bn} \quad SS_{wn} \quad df_{tot} \quad df_{bn} \quad df_{wn} \quad MS_{bn} \quad MS_{wn} \quad F_{obt} \quad F_{crit} \quad \sigma^2_{error} \quad \sigma^2_{treat} \quad \eta^2$

ANOVA	mean square within groups
factor	mean square between groups
level	error variance
treatment	treatment variance
treatment effect	F-ratio
one-way ANOVA	sum of squares
between-subjects factor	F-distribution
between-subjects ANOVA	Fisher's protected t-test
within-subjects factor	Tukey's HSD multiple comparisons test
within-subjects ANOVA	eta
analysis of variance	eta squared
experimentwise error rate	univariate statistics
post hoc comparisons	multivariate statistics

USING WHAT YOU KNOW

1. a. What does ANOVA stand for?
    b. What research design requires its use?
    c. What does this procedure enable us to decide?

2. a. What is a between-subjects factor?
    b. What is a within-subjects factor?
    c. What type of ANOVA is used in experiments with only one factor?

3. What are the assumptions of the one-way, between-subjects ANOVA?

4. What do H_0 and H_a maintain in the ANOVA? (Provide a description.)

5. a. What are error variance and treatment variance?
    b. What are the two types of mean squares and what does each estimate?

6. a. Why is F_{obt} greater than 1 when H_0 is false?
    b. Why is F_{obt} greater than 1 when H_0 is true?

7. Suppose we predict the mean of one level will be smaller than the mean of another level. Why can't we perform a one-tailed test in ANOVA?

8. a. Why do we perform the ANOVA in experiments with more than two conditions of the independent variable rather than simply use multiple t-tests?
    b. What is meant by the experimentwise error rate?

9. a. When is it necessary to perform post hoc comparisons and why?
    b. When is it unnecessary to perform post hoc comparisons and why?
    c. Identify the two types of post hoc tests and indicate when each is used.

10. a. What does eta squared indicate?
    b. Give the symbol for this statistic.

11. When an F-test is significant, name four additional procedures you should do.

12. Given the following information:

Source	Sum of Squares	df	Mean Square	F
Between groups	127.60	2		
Within groups	593.45	12		
Total	721.05	14		

    a. How many levels were involved?
    b. How many participants were involved?
    c. Complete the ANOVA summary table.
    d. Using $\alpha = 0.05$, what is F_{crit}?
    e. Is the F-test significant?
    f. Based on your answer in part e, what else should you do?

13. Given the following information:

$$\Sigma X_{tot} = 145 \qquad \Sigma X_1 = 32$$
$$\Sigma X_{tot}^2 = 881 \qquad \Sigma X_2 = 47$$
$$n_1 = n_2 = n_3 = 10 \qquad \Sigma X_3 = 66$$

Source	Sum of Squares	df	Mean Square	F

    a. Complete the ANOVA summary table.
    b. Using $\alpha = 0.05$, what is F_{crit}?
    c. Is the F-test significant?

14.   Katie is studying aggression among adolescent girls. She believes that there is a
       relationship between the level of interaction a girl has with her mother and the level of
       aggression. She has identified 5 girls who fall into each of 4 interaction levels and has
       measured their aggression scores. Her data are given below.

No Interaction	Low Interaction	Moderate Interaction	High Interaction
4	4	4	3
5	6	4	4
6	5	3	4
6	4	5	3
5	5	4	3

a.   What are the independent variable and the dependent variable?
b.   Should Katie conduct a between-subjects ANOVA or a within-subjects ANOVA? Explain
     your answer.
c.   How many factors are involved in Katie's study?
d.   How many levels are involved? Name the level(s).
e.   What are the H_0 and H_a?
f.   Complete the ANOVA summary table.
g.   If you use $\alpha = 0.05$, what is the appropriate F_{crit}?
h.   Is the F-test significant? Why or why not?
i.   If the F-test is significant, perform the appropriate post hoc test.
j.   What should Katie conclude based on these findings?
k.   If appropriate, calculate the effect size.
l.   If appropriate, calculate a 95% confidence interval around μ of the No Interaction group.
m.   Compute the means and graph the results.

THE TEST

1.   In a one-way ANOVA, when testing independent samples, we have a _____ factor.

     a.   between-subjects
     b.   within-subjects
     c.   significant
     d.   nonsignificant

2.   ANOVA tests are

     a.   always based on one-tailed hypotheses.
     b.   always based on two-tailed hypotheses.
     c.   sometimes based on one-tailed and sometimes based on two-tailed hypotheses.
     d.   based on two-tailed hypotheses except when we predict the direction in which the means
          should differ.

3. In a one-way, between-subjects ANOVA, F_{obt} is computed by dividing

    a. MS_{bn} by MS_{wn}.
    b. MS_{wn} by MS_{bn}.
    c. MS_{bn} by MS_{tot}.
    d. MS_{wn} by SS_{wn}.

4. If $SS_{bn} = 20$, $SS_{wn} = 50$, $k = 3$, $N = 23$, what is F_{obt}?

    a. 10
    b. 2.5
    c. 20
    d. 4.0

5. Which of the following is *not* used after the one-way ANOVA to describe a significant relationship?

    a. computing a confidence interval for each population mean
    b. graphing the relationship
    c. computing the effect size
    d. performing a series of *t*-tests on each pair of sample means

ANSWERS TO USING WHAT YOU KNOW

1. a. Analysis of variance.
   b. An experiment involving more than two levels of the independent variable.
   c. Whether the differences between two or more sample means represent differences between μs or merely reflect sampling error.

2. a. An independent variable that is studied using independent samples in each condition.
   b. An independent variable that is studied by testing related samples under all conditions.
   c. A one-way ANOVA.

3. We assume that there is only one independent variable and one dependent variable, that each condition contains a random independent sample, that the raw scores are measured using an interval or a ratio scale, and that the populations represented are normally distributed and have homogeneous variance.

4. H_0 maintains that all μs represented by the levels are equal; H_a maintains that not all μs represented by the levels are equal.

5. a. Error variance is the inherent variability or differences between scores in each population. Treatment variance is variability between scores in the different populations created by the different levels of the factor.
   b. The mean square within groups, which estimates the error variance; and the mean square between groups, which estimates the error variance plus the treatment variance.

6. a. Differences between the sample means reflect treatment variance plus error variance; therefore, MS_{bn} is greater than MS_{wn} and their ratio equals a value greater than 1.
    b. MS_{bn} contains sampling error in representing the same value as MS_{wn}, and so F_{obt} is greater than 1 because of sampling error.

7. Regardless of whether the mean is smaller or larger than the other mean, the value of F_{obt} will be greater than 1.0.

8. a. Multiple *t*-tests do not control the experimentwise error rate so that it equals our α. The ANOVA does.
    b. The overall probability of making a Type I error after comparing all means in an experiment. The more significance tests you compute, the more likely it is that one of them will reach the critical value and be declared "significant" due to sampling error rather than because of an actual difference.

9. a. When F_{obt} is significant and k is greater than 2, because the F_{obt} indicates only that two or more sample means differ significantly; therefore, post hoc tests are used to determine which specific levels produced significant differences.
    b. When F_{obt} is not significant, because we are not convinced that there are any differences to be found. Also, when $k = 2$, because there is only one possible difference between means in the study.
    c. Fisher's protected *t*-test, used when F_{obt} is significant, when there are more than two levels, and when the *n*s in all conditions are not equal. Tukey's *HSD* test, used when F_{obt} is significant, when there are more than two levels, and when the *n*s in all conditions are equal.

10. a. It indicates the effect size, or the proportion of variance in dependent scores accounted for by changing the levels of the independent variable.
    b. The symbol for eta squared is η^2.

11. a. Conduct a post hoc analysis
    b. Generate a graph
    c. Compute the effect size
    d. Determine the confidence interval for each population mean

12. a. $k = 3$
    b. $N = 15$
    c.

Source	Sum of Squares	df	Mean Square	F
Between groups	127.60	2	63.80	1.290
Within groups	593.45	12	49.454	
Total	721.05	14		

d. $F_{crit} = 3.88$

e.   No, the F-test is not significant.

f.   Because the F-test is not significant, no other procedures should be performed.

13.   a.

Source	Sum of Squares	df	Mean Square	F
Between groups	58.067	2	29.034	6.421
Within groups	122.10	27	4.522	
Total	180.167	29		

$$SS_{tot} = 881 - \left(\frac{145^2}{30}\right) = 180.167$$

$$SS_{bn} = \Sigma\left(\frac{32^2}{10} + \frac{47^2}{10} + \frac{66^2}{10}\right) - \left(\frac{145^2}{30}\right) = 58.067$$

$$SS_{wn} = 180.167 - 58.067 = 122.10$$

$$df_{bn} = 3 - 1 = 2$$

$$df_{wn} = 30 - 3 = 27$$

$$df_{tot} = 30 - 1 = 29 = 2 + 27$$

$$MS_{bn} = \frac{58.067}{2} = 29.034$$

$$MS_{wn} = \frac{122.10}{27} = 4.522$$

$$F_{obt} = \frac{29.034}{4.522} = 6.421$$

b. $F_{crit} = 3.35$

c.   Yes, the F-test is significant.

14.   a.   The independent variable is the level of interaction with the mother. The dependent variable is the aggression score.

b.   She should do a between-subject ANOVA because the scores are independent.

c.   There is one factor (i.e., the independent variable). It is the level of interaction with the mother.

d.   There are four levels—No Interaction, Low Interaction, Moderate Interaction, and High Interaction.

e. $H_0 : \mu_1 = \mu_2 = \mu_3$
H_a : not all the μ s are equal.

f.

Source	Sum of Squares	df	Mean Square	F
Between groups	9.75	3	3.250	5.91
Within groups	8.80	16	0.550	
Total	18.85	19		

$$SS_{tot} = 397 - \left(\frac{87^2}{20}\right) = 18.55$$

$$SS_{bn} = \left(\frac{26^2}{5} + \frac{24^2}{5} + \frac{20^2}{5} + \frac{17^2}{5}\right) - \left(\frac{87^2}{20}\right) = 9.75$$

$$SS_{wn} = 18.55 - 9.75 = 8.8$$

g. $F_{crit} = 3.24$

h. Yes. Because $F(3,16) = 5.91$ which is greater than F_{crit}.

i. Because all ns are equal, the Tukey HSD multiple comparison test is appropriate.

$$k = 4, df_{wn} = 16, \text{ and } \alpha = 0.05, \text{so } q_k = 4.05$$

$$\overline{X}_1 = 5.20; \overline{X}_2 = 4.80; \overline{X}_3 = 4.00; \overline{X}_4 = 3.40$$

$$HSD = 4.05\left(\sqrt{\frac{0.550}{5}}\right) = 1.343$$

$$\overline{X}_1 - \overline{X}_2 = 0.40 \quad \overline{X}_2 - \overline{X}_3 = 0.80 \quad \overline{X}_3 - \overline{X}_4 = 0.60$$

$$\overline{X}_1 - \overline{X}_3 = 1.20 \quad \overline{X}_2 - \overline{X}_4 = 1.40$$

$$\overline{X}_1 - \overline{X}_4 = 3.00$$

j. Katie should conclude that the mean of the No Interaction group is significantly different from the mean of the High Interaction group and that the mean of the Low Interaction group also is significantly different from the mean of the High Interaction group. No other differences exist among the group means.

k. $\eta^2 = \dfrac{9.75}{18.85} = 0.52$

l. $\left(\sqrt{\dfrac{0.550}{5}}\right)(-2.120) + 5.20 \leq \mu \leq \left(\sqrt{\dfrac{0.550}{5}}\right)(2.120) + 5.20 = 4.50 \leq \mu \leq 5.90$

m.

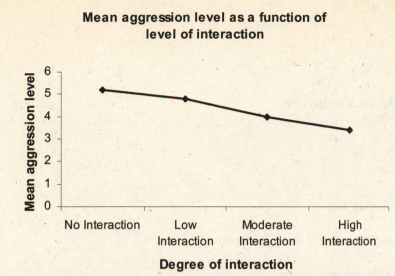

Mean aggression level as a function of level of interaction

ANSWERS TO THE TEST

1. a   2. b   3. a   4. d   5. d

Chapter 14
The Two-Way Analysis of Variance

YOU SHOULD LEARN

1. What a two-way factorial ANOVA is.

2. How to collapse across a factor to find main effect means.

3. How to find the cell means for the interaction.

4. How the three Fs in a two-way ANOVA are computed.

5. What a significant main effect indicates.

6. What a significant interaction indicates.

7. How to perform post hoc tests, compute η^2, and graph each effect.

8. How to interpret the results from a two-way experiment.

YOU SHOULD LEARN WHEN, WHY, AND HOW TO USE THESE FORMULAS

1. The formula for the SS_{tot} is

$$SS_{tot} = \Sigma X_{tot}^2 - \left(\frac{(\Sigma X_{tot})^2}{N} \right)$$

2. The formula for the sum of squares between groups for the column Factor A is

$$SS_A = \Sigma \left(\frac{(\text{Sum of scores in the column})^2}{n \text{ of scores in the column}} \right) - \left(\frac{(\Sigma X_{tot})^2}{N} \right)$$

3. The formula for the sum of squares between groups for the row Factor B is

$$SS_B = \Sigma \left(\frac{(\text{Sum of scores in the row})^2}{n \text{ of scores in the row}} \right) - \left(\frac{(\Sigma X_{tot})^2}{N} \right)$$

4. The formula for the sum of squares between groups is

$$SS_{bn} = \sum \left(\frac{(\text{Sum of scores in the cell})^2}{n \text{ of scores in the cell}} \right) - \left(\frac{(\Sigma X_{tot})^2}{N} \right)$$

The SS_{bn} is then used in the formula for the sum of squares between groups for the interaction, A x B.

$$SS_{AxB} = SS_{bn} - SS_A - SS_B$$

5. The formula for the sum of squares within groups is

$$SS_{wn} = SS_{tot} - SS_{bn}$$

6. To compute the degrees of freedom,

$$df_A = k_A - 1 \qquad \text{where } k_A \text{ is the number of levels in Factor A.}$$

$$df_B = k_B - 1 \qquad \text{where } k_B \text{ is the number of levels in Factor B.}$$

$$df_{AxB} = (df_A)(df_B)$$

$$df_{wn} = N - k_{AxB} \qquad \text{where } N \text{ is the total } N \text{ of the study and } k_{AxB} \text{ is the total number of cells in the study.}$$

7. The formulas for the mean squares are

$$MS_A = \frac{SS_A}{df_A} \qquad\qquad MS_B = \frac{SS_B}{df_B}$$

$$MS_{AxB} = \frac{SS_{AxB}}{df_{AxB}} \qquad\qquad MS_{wn} = \frac{SS_{wn}}{df_{wn}}$$

8. The formulas for F_{obt} are

$$F_A = \frac{MS_A}{MS_{wn}} \qquad F_B = \frac{MS_B}{MS_{wn}} \qquad F_{AxB} = \frac{MS_{AxB}}{MS_{wn}}$$

Values of F_{crit} are found in Table 5 of Appendix C. To find F_{crit} to test F_A, use df_A and df_{wn}. To find F_{crit} to test F_B, use df_B and df_{wn}. To find F_{crit} to test F_{AxB}, use df_{AxB} and df_{wn}.

9. The formula for Tukey's *HSD* is

$$HSD = (q_k)\left(\sqrt{\frac{MS_{wn}}{n}}\right)$$

where n is the number of scores used to compute each mean being compared.

Values of q_k are found in the textbook appendices (Table C.6).

For main effects, k equals the number of levels in the factor. For the interaction, k equals the adjusted value, as indicated in the following table:

Values of Adjusted k

Design of Study	Number of Cell Means in Study	Adjusted Value of k
2 x 2	4	3
2 x 3	6	5
2 x 4	8	6
3 x 3	9	7
3 x 4	12	8
4 x 4	16	10
4 x 5	20	12

10. The formula for eta squared is

$$\eta^2 = \frac{\text{Sum of squares for the effect}}{SS_{tot}}$$

11. The formula for a confidence interval for a single μ is

$$\left(\sqrt{\frac{MS_{wn}}{n}}\right)(-t_{crit}) + \overline{X} \leq \mu \leq \left(\sqrt{\frac{MS_{wn}}{n}}\right)(+t_{crit}) + \overline{X}$$

where t_{crit} is the two-tailed value at $df = df_{wn}$.

ONE MORE TIME: A Review

	When an experiment contains two independent variables, we may perform
two-way	the _____ - _____ ANOVA. In the two-way between-subjects
independent	ANOVA, we assume that each cell has _____ samples, that the

dependent variable is measured using a(n) _____ scale or a(n) | interval

_____ scale and that the populations represented form _____ | ratio; normal

distributions with _____ variances. | homogeneous

We describe ANOVA using the format "A x B," where A and B stand

for the number of _____ in Factor A and Factor B, respectively. When | levels

all levels of one factor are combined with all levels of the other factor, we

have a complete _____ design. Each specific condition produced by | factorial

the combination of a level of Factor A with a level of Factor B is called a(n)

_____. | cell

We perform the two-way, between-subjects ANOVA when all cells

involve _____ samples. If all cells involve related samples, we | independent

perform the two-way, _____ - _____ ANOVA. If one factor is a | within-subjects

between-subjects factor and the other factor is a within-subjects factor, we

perform the _____ - _____ ANOVA. | mixed-design

In a two-factor experiment, we examine both the _____ effects | main

and the _____ effect. When we examine the effect of changing the | interaction

levels of one factor, ignoring the other factor, we are examining the

_____ _____ of the factor. In a two-way ANOVA, the number | main effect

of main effects is _____. When we examine the combined effect of | two

changing the levels of both factors, we are examining the _____ effect. | interaction

Overview of the Two-Way, Between-Subjects ANOVA

The very first step in the two-way ANOVA is to set up our _____. For | hypotheses

the main effect of Factor A, the null hypothesis states the means for each

_____ of Factor A (_____ across Factor B) are _____. | level; collapsing; equal

The alternative hypothesis says not all the _____ are equal. For the | means

means

A

interaction

depends

no; alternative

is

Factor B

collapsing

Factor A

one

relationship

F_A

two

one

F_B; two

different

main effect of Factor B, the _____ hypothesis indicates equality of the

_____ across all levels of Factor B (collapsing across Factor

_____).

    The third term in a two- way ANOVA is the two-way _____. If

an interaction is present, how much one of the factors influences the scores

_____ on the level of the other factor. The null hypothesis for the

interaction term states _____ interaction is present. The _____

hypothesis says there _____ an interaction.

    To compute the main effect means for Factor A, we compute the mean

for each level of Factor A using the scores for all participants in that level,

averaging across all levels of _____ _____. Averaging across all

levels of Factor B is called _____ across the levels of Factor B. To

compute the main effect means of Factor B, we collapse across the levels of

_____ _____.

    We test the main effect of changing the levels of Factor A by testing

the H_0 the main effect means from Factor A represent _____

population μ_A and, therefore, do not represent a(n) _____. To test

H_0 for Factor A, we compute _____. If F_A is significant, we conclude

at least _____ means differ significantly. Likewise, we test whether

there is an effect of changing the levels of Factor B by testing the H_0 that the

main effect means from B represent _____ population μ_B. We compute

_____. If it is significant, we conclude at least _____ of the

means of Factor B represent _____ μs.

Finally, we test the _____ effect by testing the H_0 each _____ | interaction; cell

mean represents the same μ_{AxB}. To test the interaction effect, we compute

_____. If it is significant, then (1) the effect of changing the levels of | F_{AxB}

one factor is not _____ for each level of the other factor; (2) the effect | consistent

of changing the levels of one factor _____ on which level of the other | depends

factor we are examining; (3) the relationship between one factor and the

dependent variable _____ as we change the levels of the other factor; | changes

and (4) when graphed, the lines are not _____. | parallel

Computing the Two-Way ANOVA

As in any F_{obt}, the MS_{wn} estimates the _____ variance in the | error

population, which reflects the inherent _____ in scores in the raw | differences

score populations represented by our samples. We compute MS_{wn} by

computing the "average" of the variability of the scores in the _____. | cells

We estimate the variance between groups by computing a(n) _____ | mean

_____ between groups. This measures the differences between the | square

_____ as an estimate of both the error variance and the _____ | means; treatment

variance in the population. We partition the between-groups variance into the

variance resulting from each _____ effect and the _____. | main; interaction

Therefore, we compute a total of _____ mean squares between groups. | three

    The first components we must compute are the _____ | sums

_____ _____. We compute the sum of squares between groups | of squares

for Factor A, symbolized as _____; the sum of squares between groups | SS_A

for Factor B, symbolized as _____; and the sum of squares between | SS_B

groups for the interaction, symbolized as _____. Finally, we compute | SS_{AxB}

the sum of squares within groups, symbolized as _____. | SS_{wn}

level	When we calculate the SS_A, we find the sum of scores for each _____
B	of Factor A, ignoring the level of Factor _____ the individual may
sum	have received. To calculate the SS_B, we find the _____ of scores for
Factor A	each level of Factor B, ignoring the level of _____ _____. For
between	the SS_{AxB}, we first find the sum of squares _____ groups and then
SS_B	subtract the SS_A and the _____ from it.
N	The degrees of freedom total equals _____ – 1, where
N	_____ is the total number of scores in the study. The degrees of
$k_A - 1$	freedom between groups for the main effect of Factor A is _____
k_A; levels	where _____ is the number of _____ in Factor A. Likewise the
	degrees of freedom between groups for the main effect of Factor B is
$k_B - 1$; k_B; Factor	_____ where _____ is the number of levels of _____
B	_____.To find the degrees of freedom between groups for the
df; multiply	interaction, we take the _____ for Factor A and _____ by the
df	_____ for Factor B. And last, but not least, the degrees of freedom
$N - k_{AxB}$	within groups is equal to _____ where N is the total N of the study and
k_{AxB}; cells	_____ is the number of _____ in the study.
mean squares	Next, we compute the _____ _____. For Factor A, we
SS_A; df_A; MS_A	divide _____ by _____ to obtain _____. For Factor B,
SS_B; df_B; MS_B	we divide _____ by _____ to obtain _____. For the
SS_{AxB}; df_{AxB}; MS_{AxB}	interaction we divide _____ by _____ to obtain _____.
SS_{wn}; df_{wn}	For the error term, we divide _____ by _____ to obtain
MS_{wn}; F_{obt}	_____. Finally, we compute _____. For Factor A, dividing
MS_A; MS_{wn}; F_A	_____ by _____ yields _____. For Factor B, dividing

_____ by MS_{wn} yields _____. For the interaction, dividing

MS_B; F_B

_____ by MS_{wn} yields _____.

MS_{AxB}; F_{AxB}

To summarize and keep track of these components we create a

_____ _____.

summary table

Interpreting Each F

We must now obtain _____. We find each F_{crit} in the F-table using

F_{crit}

df_A, df_B, or df_{AxB} and the value of _____. For each F_{obt}, if H_0 is

df_{wn}

true, there should be no _____ variance resulting from that effect, and

treatment

thus F_{obt} should equal _____. The larger the F_{obt}, the _____

1; less

likely it is that H_0 is true and the means from the factor represent

_____ μ. If F_{obt} is significant, then we conclude at least _____

one; two

means in that factor represent _____ μs. Thus, if F_A is significant, we

different

are _____ Factor A would produce a relationship in the _____.

confident; population

Likewise, if F_B is significant, we conclude a relationship exists between the

_____ variable scores and the _____ of Factor B. With a

dependent; levels

significant interaction, we are confident the relationship between the scores

and the levels of Factor A _____ on the particular level of Factor B

depends

under which subjects are tested.

If an F_{obt} is not larger than its F_{crit}, we fail to _____ H_0 for that

reject

effect and conclude the corresponding means may represent _____

one

population μ. Therefore, we have insufficient evidence to indicate the

variable is involved in a(n) _____ in the population. To understand the

relationship

means; post

hoc

specifics of each relationship reflected by a significant F_{obt}, we must

determine which _____ differ significantly by performing _____

_____ comparisons.

Interpreting the Two-Way Experiment

interaction

graph; separately

mean; post hoc

not; cell

main; most

dependent

line

parallel

significant; 2

For each significant main effect and _____, we should generate a

_____. Each main effect is graphed _____. In these, we plot

every _____, even if the _____ _____ test says it is

_____ significant. To graph the interaction, we plot each _____

mean. On the X axis, we put the _____ effect with the _____

levels. The Y axis contains the _____ variable. Each level of the

remaining factor is graphed on its own _____. If there is an interaction

present, the lines will not be _____.

We perform a post hoc test if F_{obt} is _____ and $k >$ _____.

Fisher's *t*-test

Tukey's *HSD*

If the *n*s in all levels of a factor are not equal, then we compare all pairs of

means using the _____ _____. If the *n*s in all levels of the factor

are equal, we compute _____ _____. We compute a different

value of *HSD* for each significant effect. This may involve a different value

k; n

of _____ and/or _____ for each significant effect.

For each significant main effect, we first find the value of q_k in the

means

textbook appendices, where *k* is the number of _____ in the factor.

We compute *HSD* with *n* equal to the number of scores that went into each

mean; difference

pair

greater

_____ we are comparing. Then we find the _____ between

every _____ of means in the effect. If the difference between two

means is _____ than the *HSD*, then those means differ significantly.

For a significant interaction, we first determine the _____ value | adjusted

of k and then find _____. We compute HSD, with n equal to the | q_k

number of scores in each _____. Next, we find the differences between | cell

all pairs of cell means that fall into the same _____ or into the same | row

_____ in the diagram of the study. In this way, we make only | column

_____ comparisons. If we compare means from cells that lie | unconfounded

diagonally to each other, we are making a(n) _____ comparison. | confounded

Confounded means are a problem because the cells differ along more than

one _____. Any two unconfounded cell means that differ by an | factor

amount _____ than HSD are _____ different. | greater; significantly

Interpreting the Overall Results of the Experiment

To interpret the overall results of the ANOVA, we look at the significant

_____ _____ comparisons within the _____ main effects | post hoc; significant

and interaction. For each main effect, we then describe the manner in which

the _____ variable changed as we changed those levels of the factor | dependent

that were _____ different. Here, we make an overall conclusion about | significantly

the factor, while _____ the other factor. | ignoring

Our conclusions about main effects may be untrue if we have a(n)

_____ _____. The interaction indicates the manner in which the | significant interaction

scores change as we change the levels of Factor A _____ on which | depends

level of Factor _____ we are talking about, and vice versa. Because | B

the interaction may contradict the pattern suggested by each main effect, we

_____ make a(n) _____ conclusion about the main effect when | cannot; overall

the interaction is significant. In general, we must limit our interpretation of a

study to the significant _____ effect. When the interaction is not | interaction

| main | significant, then we focus on any significant _____ effects. Because |

interactions can be very difficult to interpret, the conventional wisdom is to

three limit a multifactor study to, at most, _____ factors.

relationships The final step is to describe the _____ demonstrated by our study.

To describe the population μ represented by any significant main effect

confidence interval mean or cell mean, we can compute the _____ _____ for μ. This

$\overline{X}$ describes those values of μ the _____ in the level or cell is

likely _____ to represent.

significant We describe the effect size for each _____ effect by computing

η^2; **variance** _____. Each describes the proportion of _____ in the dependent

accounted; variable that is _____ for by the _____ variable in that effect.
independent

consistently The larger the η^2, the more _____ the scores changed as we changed

the levels of the independent variable or cells in the effect, and thus the

more _____ important the effect in explaining the difference in scores.

NOW DO YOU KNOW?

SS_A SS_B SS_{AxB} df_A df_B df_{AxB} df_{wn} MS_A MS_B MS_{AxB} F_A F_B F_{AxB}

two-way ANOVA
two-way between-subjects ANOVA
two-way within-subjects ANOVA
two-way mixed-design ANOVA
cell
complete factorial design
incomplete factorial design

main effect
main effect mean
collapsing
two-way interaction effect
confounded comparison
unconfounded comparison

USING WHAT YOU KNOW

1. a. What are the characteristics of an experiment that calls for a two-way, complete factorial, between-subjects ANOVA?
   b. What are the other assumptions of the two-way, between-subjects ANOVA?

2.   What is a cell?

3.   a.   What is the main effect of a factor?
     b.   How do we collapse across Factor B to compute the main effect means of A?
     c.   What does a significant main effect indicate about these means?
     d.   What is the orientation of the line graph of a significant main effect?

4.   a.   What information can be obtained from a two-way ANOVA that cannot be obtained from two one-way designs using the same variables?
     b.   How do we obtain the means that are examined in an interaction effect?
     c.   What does a significant interaction effect indicate about these means?

5.   Describe the null and alternative hypotheses for the main effects and the interaction effect in a two-way ANOVA.

6.   Identify the F-ratios computed in a two-way ANOVA.

7.   a.   Identify and define the variance estimated by the MS within groups in a two-way ANOVA.
     b.   Identify and define the variance estimated by each MS between groups in this procedure.

8.   a.   What must be done for each significant effect in a two-way ANOVA before attempting to interpret the results of an experiment?
     b.   Explain why this must be done.

9.   Why is the interpretation of the results from a two-way ANOVA limited to the interaction when it is significant?

10. Why is it wise to limit a multifactor experiment to two or three factors?

11. Complete the following ANOVA summary table.

Source	Sum of Squares	df	Mean Square	F
Between	150	5		
Factor A	80	2	☐	☐
Factor B	30	1	☐	☐
A x B Interaction	☐	☐	☐	☐
Within	☐	☐	☐	
Total	500	29		

12. a. Graph the following cell means for two experiments. Label the X-axis with Factor A.

	Study 1				Study 2		
	A_1	A_2	A_3		A_1	A_2	A_3
B_1	10	8	7	B_1	2	6	9
B_2	9	13	18	B_2	3	8	12

   b. Using the graphs you developed in part a, what would you conclude about possible AxB interactions?
   c. Using the cell means given in part a, again generate a graph but label the X axis using Factor B.
   d. Using the graphs you developed in part c, what would you now conclude about possible A x B interaction?

13. After performing a 3 x 3 ANOVA with equal ns, you find that all Fs are significant.

   a. What is your next step?
   b. What other procedures should you perform?

14. a. What is a confounded comparison?
   b. What is an unconfounded comparison?
   c. Why do we not perform confounded comparisons when performing post hoc tests of a significant interaction?

15. a. When should you compute the effect size in a two-way ANOVA?
   b. Why should you compute the effect size?

16. In a study involving the effect of amount of fat in the diet and amount of exercise on the mental acuity of middle-aged men, Dr. Parks is using three treatment levels for diet (<30% fat, 30% – 60% fat, and >60% fat) and two levels for exercise (<60 minutes per week and 60 or more minutes per week). The data from her study follow:

		Factor A		
		<30% fat	30 – 60% fat	>60% fat
	<60 minutes	4	3	2
		4	1	2
		2	2	2
		4	2	2
		3	3	1
Factor B				
	60 minutes or more	6	8	5
		5	8	7
		4	7	5
		4	8	5
		5	6	6

a. What is (are) the independent variable(s)?
b. What is (are) the dependent variable(s)?
c. How many levels does Factor A have?
d. How many levels does Factor B have?
e. How many participants received each level of Factor A?
f. How many participants received each level of Factor B?
g. How many participants received each treatment?

17. For the data given in problem 17:

a. Complete the ANOVA and create a summary table.
b. Determine which effects are significant.
c. Perform appropriate post hoc tests.
d. Compute appropriate effect sizes.
e. What conclusions should be drawn from this study?

18. A researcher examines the effects of attendance in class and completion of homework assignments on statistics test grades. Half her subjects complete 5 homework assignments, and the other half complete 15. She determines the number of absences for each participant and assigns each to either the low- or high-absenteeism condition. From the 10 people per cell, she obtains the following mean test scores and sums of squares:

Factor A
Absenteeism

		Low	High	
Factor B	5	8.7	6.4	7.6
Homeworks	15	9.4	8.6	9.0
		9.1	7.5	

Summary Table of Two-Way ANOVA

Source	Sum of Squares	df	Mean Square	F
Between				
Factor A	25.60			
Factor B	22.50			
Interaction	5.63			
Within	35.25			
Total	88.98			

a. Complete the ANOVA and create a summary table.
b. Determine which effects are significant.
c. Perform the appropriate post hoc comparisons.
d. Compute the effect size where appropriate.
e. What conclusions can be drawn from this study?

19. a. When is a two-way, within-subjects ANOVA performed?
    b. When is a two-way, mixed-design ANOVA performed?

THE TEST

1. A two-way between-subjects ANOVA is performed when you have

    a. . related samples in all cells.
    b. more than two levels in each factor.
    c. independent samples in all cells.
    d. one repeated measures factor and one factor with independent samples.

2. When the effect on scores of changing the levels of one factor depends on which level of the other factor you examine, you have

    a. a significant interaction effect.
    b. two significant main effects.
    c. a single significant main effect with no interaction effect.
    d. a nonsignificant interaction effect and no signficant main effects.

3. When two cells differ along more than one factor, the two means are said to be

    a. significantly different.
    b. confounded.
    c. unconfounded.
    d. different due to sampling error.

4. In a two-way ANOVA, when the interaction effect is significant, the primary interpretation of the results rests on

    a. whether you have a large enough sample size.
    b. whether you can really meet the assumptions.
    c. the interpretation of any significant main effects.
    d. the interpretation of the interaction.

5. Which term is used as the denominator to calculate F_{AxB}?

    a. df_{AxB}
    b. SS_{AxB}
    c. MS_{AxB}
    d. MS_{wn}

ANSWERS TO USING WHAT YOU KNOW

1. a. The experiment has two independent variables, with all levels of one factor combined with all levels of the other factor, in which independent samples are used.
    b. We assume that the scores are measured using interval or ratio scales and that the populations represented are normally distributed and have homogeneous variance.

2. A treatment condition resulting from the combination of a level of one factor with a level of the other factor.

3. a. The effect of changing the levels of that factor on the dependent variable scores.
    b. We average together all scores from all levels of Factor B so that we have the mean for each level of A.
    c. It indicates that at least two of the means are likely to represent different μs.
    d. The line will not be horizontal.

4. a. The effect of the interaction of the two variables.
    b. By computing the mean of each cell, not collapsing across either factor.
    c. It indicates that they represent a pattern of μs in the population in which the relationship between one factor and the dependent scores changes as the levels of the other factor change.

5. For each main effect, H_0 maintains that the μs represented by the levels of the factor are all equal; H_a states that not all μs are equal. For the interaction, H_0 states that the μs represented by the cells do not form an interaction; H_a states that the μs do form an interaction.

6. The F for the main effect of Factor A, the F for the main effect of Factor B, and the F for the interaction of Factors A and B.

7. a. The error variance—the variability of scores within each population of scores.
    b. The error variance plus the treatment variance for Factor A—the differences attributable to Factor A; the error variance plus the treatment variance for Factor B—the differences attributable to Factor B; and the error variance plus the treatment variance for A x B—the differences attributable to the interaction.

8. a. Post hoc comparisons, when appropriate, must be performed.
    b. To determine which specific levels or cells in the factor or interaction differ significantly.

9. The interaction contradicts any general conclusion drawn from a main effect because the interaction indicates that the effect of one variable depends on the levels of the other factor.

10. The complexity of the interaction increases dramatically with more than three factors, so that it is usually virtually uninterpretable.

11.

Source	Sum of Squares	df	Mean Square	F
Between	150	5		
Factor A	80	2	40	2.74
Factor B	30	1	30	2.06
A x B Interaction	40	2	20	1.37
Within	350	24	14.58	
Total	500			

12.   a.

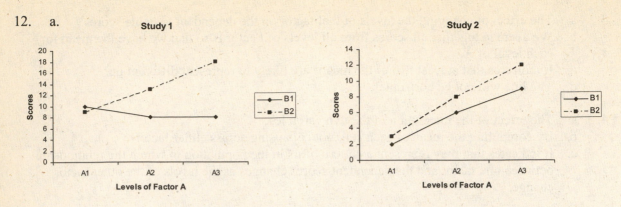

b.   In Study 1,there does appear to be an A x B Interaction. In Study 2, there does not appear to
      be an A x B Interaction.

c.

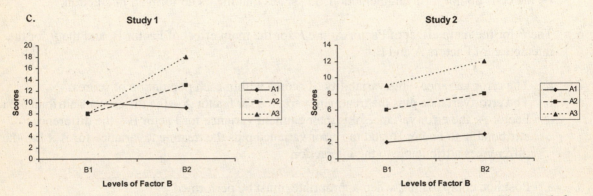

d.   Again, the graph for Study 1 indicates the presence of an A x B interaction. The graph for
      Study 2 does not indicate the presence of an interaction.

13.   a.   Perform Tukey's post hoc comparisons on each factor.
       b.   Graph each significant effect and compute its η^2; where appropriate, compute confidence
             intervals for the μ represented by a cell or level mean.

14.   a.   When two cells differ along more than one factor.
       b.   When two cells differ along only one factor.
       c.   Because we would not be able to determine which of the two factors produced the
             difference between the cell means.

15.   a.   Compute η^2 for each significant main effect and interaction effect.
       b.   To determine the proportion of the total variance in dependent variable scores accounted
             for by changing the levels of a significant main effect or the cells of the significant
             interaction.

16.   a.   Amount of fat in the diet and amount of exercise
       b.   Mental acuity
       c.   3 levels
       d.   2 levels
       c.   10 participants
       d.   15 participants
       e.   5 participants

17. a. $SS_{tot} = 660 - \dfrac{126^2}{30} = 130.80$

$SS_A = \left(\dfrac{41^2}{10} + \dfrac{48^2}{10} + \dfrac{37^2}{10}\right) - \dfrac{126^2}{30} = 6.20$

$SS_B = \left(\dfrac{37^2}{15} + \dfrac{89^2}{15}\right) - \dfrac{126^2}{30} = 90.133$

$SS_{bn} = \left(\dfrac{17^2}{5} + \dfrac{11^2}{5} + \dfrac{9^2}{5} + \dfrac{24^2}{5} + \dfrac{37^2}{5} + \dfrac{28^2}{5}\right) - \dfrac{126^2}{30} = 114.80$

$SS_{AxB} = 114.80 - 6.20 - 90.133 = 18.467$

$SS_{wn} = 130.80 - 114.80 = 16.0$

$df_A = 3 - 1 = 2$; $df_B = 2 - 1 = 1$; $df_{AxB} = (2)(1) = 2$; $df_{wn} = 30 - 6 = 24$

$MS_A = \dfrac{6.20}{2} = 3.10$; $MS_B = \dfrac{90.133}{1} = 90.133$; $MS_{AxB} = \dfrac{18.467}{2} = 9.234$

$MS_{wn} = \dfrac{16.0}{24.0} = 0.667$

$F_A = \dfrac{3.10}{0.667} = 4.648$; $F_B = \dfrac{90.133}{0.667} = 135.132$; $F_{AxB} = \dfrac{9.234}{0.667} = 13.844$

Source	Sum of Squares	df	Mean Square	F
Between	114.800			
Factor A	6.200	2	3.100	4.65
Factor B	90.133	1	90.133	135.13
A x B interaction	18.467	2	9.234	13.84
Within	16.000	24	0.667	
Total	130.800	29		

b. $F_{2,24} = 3.40$

$F_{1,24} = 4.26$

4.648 > 3.40 so Factor A is significant, $p < 0.05$.
135.132 > 4.26 so Factor B is significant, $p < 0.05$.
13.844 > 3.40 so the A x B interaction is significant, $p < 0.05$.

c.

	Cell Means		
	<30% fat	30% - 60% fat	>60% fat
<60 minutes	3.40	2.20	1.80
60 or more minutes	4.80	7.40	5.60

For Factor A, $HSD = 3.53\sqrt{\dfrac{0.667}{10}} = 0.912$

<30% fat	30% - 60% fat	>60% fat
4.10	4.80	3.70

The 30% - 60% fat group is significantly different from the >60% fat group.

For factor B, since there are only two levels no post hoc test needs to be conducted. The <60 minute group is significantly different from the 60 or more minute group.

<60 minutes	60 or more minutes
2.47	5.93

For A x B, adjusted $k = 5$ and $HSD = 4.17\sqrt{\dfrac{0.667}{5}} = 1.523$.

1. $B_1 : A_1$ vs. A_2 $3.40 - 2.20 = 1.20$
2. $B_1 : A_2$ vs. A_3 $2.20 - 1.80 = 0.40$
3. $B_1 : A_1$ vs. A_3 $3.40 - 1.80 = 1.60$
4. $B_2 : A_1$ vs. A_2 $7.40 - 4.80 = 2.60$
5. $B_2 : A_2$ vs. A_3 $7.40 - 5.60 = 1.80$
6. $B_2 : A_1$ vs. A_3 $5.60 - 4.80 = 0.80$
7. $A_1 : B_1$ vs. B_2 $4.80 - 3.40 = 1.40$
8. $A_2 : B_1$ vs. B_2 $7.40 - 2.20 = 5.20$
9. $A_3 : B_1$ vs. B_2 $5.60 - 1.80 = 3.80$

Therefore, the <30% fat group is significantly different from the > 60% fat group where participants exercised less than 60 minutes. The <30% fat group is significantly different from the 30% - 60% fat group, and the 30% - 60% group is significantly different from the >60% group where participants exercised for 60 minutes or more. Also, the group that exercised less than 60 minutes differed significantly from the group that exercised for 60 minutes or longer both when the diet consisted of 30% - 60% fat and when the diet consisted of more than 60% fat.

d. For Factor A, $\eta^2 = \dfrac{6.20}{130.80} = 0.05$

For Factor B, $\eta^2 = \dfrac{90.133}{130.80} = 0.69$

For the A x B interaction, $\eta^2 = \dfrac{18.467}{130.80} = 0.14$

e. Since the interaction is significant, we can conclude that the level of mental acuity depends on the specific combination of fat in the diet and amount of exercise. For those individuals with more than 30% fat in their diet, exercising for 60 or more minutes significantly improves mental acuity.

18. a.   Summary Table of Two-Way ANOVA

Source	Sum of Squares	df	Mean Square	F
Between				
Factor A	25.60	1	25.60	26.12
Factor B	22.50	1	22.50	22.96
Interaction	5.63	1	5.63	5.74
Within	35.25	36	0.98	
Total	88.98	39		

b. For $df = 1,36$, $F_{crit} = 4.11$. All effects are significant, $p < 0.05$.

c. Adjusted $k = 3$, $HSD = (3.46)\left(\left(\sqrt{0.98/10}\right)\right) = 1.08$. For 5 homeworks, low and high differ; for high absenteeism, 5 and 15 differ; $p < 0.05$.

d. For A, $\eta^2 = 0.29$; for B, $\eta^2 = 0.25$; for A x B, $\eta^2 = 0.06$.

e. The interaction is such that high absenteeism with 5 homeworks produced the lowest mean test score, with no significant differences between the other conditions. Arguably, with such a small η^2 for the interaction, the main effects should also be emphasized.

19. a. When the data are appropriate for a parametric procedure, there are two factors, and all cells involve related samples.

b. When the data are appropriate for a parametric procedure, there are two factors, and one factor is a between-subjects factor (with independent samples) and the other is a within-subjects factor (with related samples).

ANSWERS TO THE TEST

1. c   2. a   3. b   4. d   5. d

Chapter 15
Chi Square and Other Nonparametric Procedures

YOU SHOULD LEARN

1. The type of data that require the use of nonparametric statistics.

2. The logic and use of the one-way chi square.

3. The logic and use of the two-way chi square.

4. How to perform and interpret the nonparametric procedures corresponding to the independent samples t-test, the related samples t-test, and the one-way between-subjects and within-subjects ANOVA.

YOU SHOULD LEARN WHEN, WHY, AND HOW TO USE THESE FORMULAS

1. The formula for chi square is

$$\chi^2_{obt} = \Sigma \left(\frac{(f_o - f_e)^2}{f_e} \right)$$

In a one-way chi square when testing no difference, $f_e = N/k$ and $df = k - 1$.

In a two-way chi square, the formula for each expected frequency is

$$f_e = \frac{(\text{Cell's row total } f_o)(\text{Cell's column total } f_o)}{N}$$

$df = (\text{number of rows} - 1)(\text{number of columns} - 1)$.

2. The formulas for the phi coefficient and the contingency coefficient are

$$\Phi = \sqrt{\frac{\chi^2_{obt}}{N}} \quad \text{and} \quad C = \sqrt{\frac{\chi^2_{obt}}{N + \chi^2_{obt}}}$$

3.   The formulas for the Mann-Whitney U test are

$$U_1 = (n_1)(n_2) + \frac{n_1(n_1 + 1)}{2} - \Sigma R_1$$

and

$$U_2 = (n_1)(n_2) + \frac{n_2(n_2 + 1)}{2} - \Sigma R_2$$

Values of U_{crit} are found in Table C.8 of the textbook appendices. (U_{obt} is significant if it is *equal to or less than* U_{crit}.)

4.   The formula for the rank sums test is

$$z_{obt} = \frac{\Sigma R - \Sigma R_{exp}}{\sqrt{\dfrac{(n_1)(n_2)(N + 1)}{12}}}$$

where ΣR_{exp} is found using

$$\Sigma R_{exp} = \frac{n_1(N + 1)}{2}$$

Values of z_{crit} are found in Table C.1 of the textbook appendices.

5.   The formula for the Wilcoxon T is

$$T_{obt} = \Sigma R$$

For a two-tailed test, ΣR is the *smaller* of the sum of ranks from either the positive or the negative difference scores. For a one-tailed test, ΣR is the *predicted smallest* ΣR. Values of T_{crit} are found in Table C.9 of the textbook appendices for N = number of nonzero difference scores (T is significant if it is *equal to or less than* T_{crit}).

6.   The formula for the Kruskal-Wallis H test is

$$H_{obt} = \left(\frac{12}{N(N + 1)}\right)(SS_{bn}) - 3(N + 1)$$

where SS_{bn} is found using

$$SS_{bn} = \frac{(\Sigma R_1)^2}{n_1} + \frac{(\Sigma R_2)^2}{n_2} + \cdots + \frac{(\Sigma R_k)^2}{n_k}$$

Values of H_{crit} are found in Table C.7 of the textbook appendices, for $df = k - 1$. Post hoc comparisons are performed using the rank sums test.

7. The formula for the Friedman χ^2 test is

$$\chi^2_{obt} = \left(\frac{12}{(k)(N)(k+1)} \right)(SS_{bn}) - 3(N)(k+1)$$

where SS_{bn} is found using

$$SS_{bn} = (\Sigma R_1)^2 + (\Sigma R_2)^2 + \cdots + (\Sigma R_k)^2$$

Values of χ^2_{crit} are found in Table C.7 of the textbook appendices, for $df = k - 1$.

Post hoc comparisons are performed with Nemenyi's procedure using the formula

$$\sqrt{\left[\frac{k(k+1)}{6(N)} \right](\chi^2_{crit})}$$

8. The formulas for η^2 are

Rank Sums Test	Kruskal-Wallis H	Friedman χ^2
$\eta^2 = \dfrac{(z_{obt})^2}{N-1}$	$\eta^2 = \dfrac{H_{obt}}{N-1}$	$\eta^2 = \dfrac{\chi^2_{obt}}{(N)(k)-1}$

ONE MORE TIME: A Review

parametric

procedures

normally;
homogeneous
interval; ratio

I

larger

nonparametric

Throughout the preceding chapters, we have performed _____

_____. These assume the represented raw score populations are

_____ distributed, all population variances are _____, and the

dependent variable uses a(n) _____ scale or a(n) _____ scale. If

we use a parametric procedure when we seriously violate these assumptions,

the actual probability of a Type _____ error will be substantially

_____ than our α. Therefore, in such instances, we turn to

_____ procedures. However, we should be aware that nonparametric

procedures are less _____ than parametric procedures. This means we	powerful
are less likely to conclude a relationship exists when, in fact, one	
_____ exist, and so we are more likely to make a Type _____	does; II
error.	
We use nonparametric procedures whenever the _____ or the	median
_____ is the appropriate measure of central tendency. This occurs	mode
when we have _____ or _____ scores, or when we have	nominal; ordinal
transformed interval or ratio scores to ranked scores because the	
interval/ratio scores were from very _____ or otherwise _____	skewed; nonnormal
distributions or the samples had significantly _____ variances.	heterogeneous

One-Way Chi Square

We use chi square when we count the _____ of participants falling in	frequency
certain _____. We test whether the frequencies in each category in the	categories
_____ represent certain frequencies in the _____. The symbol	sample; population
for the chi square statistic is _____, and it is always used to test	χ^2
_____ -tailed hypotheses.	two
When a study contains categories from one variable, we use the	
_____ - _____ chi square. We create H_0 based on a model of	one-way
how the frequencies are distributed in the population if the _____	predicted
relationship does not exist. H_0 maintains that the distribution of frequencies	
in the sample _____ represents this model. H_a maintains that the	poorly
distribution of frequencies in the population is different from the distribution	
described by _____. The one-way chi square test is called a(n)	H_0

goodness of fit; well	_____ _____ _____ test because it tests how _____
fit	our data represent or "_____" the H_0 model.
	We test H_0 by determining the probability of obtaining the sample
frequencies	_____ if they represent the distribution in the population described by
	H_0. In the sample, the frequencies of participants falling into each category
observed; f_o	are called the _____ frequencies, symbolized as _____. We
expected	compare the f_o in each category to the _____ frequencies, symbolized
f_e	as _____. Each f_e is the expected number of participants in a category
perfectly; H_0	if the data _____ represent the distribution described by _____.
	The assumptions of the one-way χ^2 are (1) the independent variable is a(n)
nominal; frequency	_____ variable and the data reflect the _____ with which
category	participants fall into each _____; (2) each participant falls into
one; independent	_____ category and this is _____ of those falling into any other
responses	category; (3) the _____ of all participants are included; and (4)
5	the f_e in any category is at least _____.
	When H_0 states that there is no difference between the frequencies in the
	categories in the population, we expect the frequencies in the sample to be
equally	_____ divided among the categories. When H_0 states the frequencies
proportion	are distributed unequally, an f_e for a category equals the _____ of the
N	total that H_0 says falls into that category, multiplied by the _____ of
	the study. Either way, when H_0 is true, each f_o "should" equal the
f_e	corresponding _____. The greater the differences between
less	the f_o and f_e, the _____ likely H_0 is true.

The chi square measures the differences between _____ and | f_o

_____. In computing χ^2, we first find the _____ between f_o | f_e; difference

and f_e in a category and then _____ it. We then divide the squared | square

difference by the _____ in that category. After doing this for all | f_e

categories, we _____ the quantities. | sum

To determine if χ^2_{obt} is significant, we compare it to _____. We | χ^2_{crit}

find χ^2_{crit} in the _____ _____ tables, but to do so, we must first | chi square

compute the _____. In a one-way χ^2_{crit}, the $df =$ _____, where k | df; $k - 1$

is the number of _____. If our χ^2_{obt} is _____ than the χ^2_{crit}, the | categories; larger

results are _____. We then conclude our _____ frequencies are | significant; observed

too unlikely to accept as representative of the distribution of frequencies in

the population described by _____. Thus, we have demonstrated a | H_0

relationship in that as we change the _____, the _____ change in | categories; frequencies

the predicted fashion.

To visualize the relationship, we _____ the results. We place the | graph

_____ on the Y axis and the _____ on the X axis. Because we | frequencies; categories

have a categorical (nominal) variable, we create a(n) _____ graph. | bar

Two-Way Chi Square

We use the two-way chi square procedure when our data consist of the

frequency with which participants belong to the categories in each of

_____ variables. | two

independence

independent

dependent

depend

independent

correlation

nonsignificant;
category
predict

significant

category membership

ANOVA

cell; independent

N

f_e

f_o; row

column

row; column

N

The two-way χ^2 is a test of _____. The null hypothesis maintains the variables are _____ in the population, and the alternative hypothesis maintains the variables are _____. If the χ^2 is significant, then the frequencies in the categories of one variable _____ on which category of the other variable is being examined. If χ^2 is not significant, then category membership on one variable is _____ of category membership on the other variable. In other words, the two-way χ^2 tests whether a(n) _____ exists between the two variables. When χ^2 is _____, then no correlation exists, and so knowing the _____ participants belong to on one variable does not allow us to _____ the category they belong to on the other variable. When χ^2 is _____, then a correlation exists, and so using the categories from one variable helps us to accurately predict _____ _____ on the other variable.

To compute χ^2, we first diagram the study in the same way we diagram a(n) _____. Each f_e is then based on the probability a participant will fall into a particular _____ if the two variables are _____. By multiplying this probability by the _____ of the study, we obtain the expected frequency in the cell, which is the _____. We compute the f_e by first finding the total _____ in each _____ and in each _____. Then we compute a cell's f_e by multiplying the f_o for the _____ containing the cell by the f_o for the _____ containing the cell and then dividing by _____.

The next step is to compute _____. We then find χ^2_{crit}, using *df* equal to the quantity (_____ of _____ − 1) x (_____ of _____ − 1). According to H_0, each f_o should equal the corresponding f_e if the variables are _____. The greater the value of χ^2_{obt}, the larger the difference between _____ and _____, and so the _____ the likelihood the data poorly represent variables that are _____. A significant χ^2 indicates the observed frequencies are _____ to represent two variables that are _____ in the population. Therefore, we conclude category membership on the two variables is dependent.

When χ^2_{obt} is significant, we create a(n) _____ graph. Frequency is plotted along the _____ axis, and the categories of one variable are plotted along the _____ axis. The categories of the second variable are identified in the _____ of the graph.

A significant two-way chi square indicates a significant relationship, so we also want to describe the _____ of the relationship. To do so, we compute a statistic analogous to a(n) _____ _____. In a(n) _____ 2 x 2 chi square, we compute the _____ _____. The symbol for phi is _____. The larger the value of Φ, the more _____ membership in a category of one variable is associated with membership in a particular category of the other variable. If we square phi, the answer is analogous to _____. This indicates how much more _____ we can _____ the frequency of category membership on one variable when we know category membership on the other variable.

Right column answers: χ^2_{obt}; number; rows; number; columns; independent; f_o; f_e; lower; independent; unlikely; independent; bar; Y; X; body; strength; correlation coefficient; significant; phi coefficient; Φ; consistently; r^2; accurately; predict

significant	In a _____ two-way χ^2 other than a 2 x 2, we describe the
contingency coefficient C	strength of the relationship by computing the _____ _____. This is symbolized as _____. We interpret C in the same way we interpret
Φ ; Φ^2	_____, and C^2 is analogous to _____.

Nonparametric Procedures for Ranked Data

When we have ranked scores, we perform inferential statistics to determine

condition	whether the ranks in each _____ of the independent variable represent
population; null	different _____ of ranks. Our _____ hypothesis always implies the samples of ranks do not represent the predicted populations, whereas our
alternative	_____ hypothesis implies the samples do represent the predicted

populations.

The logic of these procedures is that if H_0 is true, then the observed sum

expected	of ranks in a condition equals the _____ sum of ranks. The symbol for
ΣR_{exp}	the expected sum of ranks is _____. In each procedure, we compute
statistic; observed	a(n) _____ that measures the difference between the _____ and
expected	_____ sum of ranks. The larger the difference between the expected
less; sampling	and observed sum of ranks, the _____ likely it is due to _____
error; less	_____, and thus the _____ likely the samples represent the

populations described by H_0. If the statistic is significant, we are confident

H_a	the observed ranks represent the population described by _____.

Each parametric procedure we have discussed has a corresponding

nonparametric	_____ procedure for ranked data. The nonparametric version of the t-test for two independent samples when each n is less than or equal to 20 is

the _____ _____ _____ test. We perform this by

computing a U for _____ sample. Then, for a two-tailed test, the value

of U_{obt} equals the _____ value of U_1 or U_2. For a one-tailed test,

U_{obt} equals the value of U_1 or U_2 we predict to be the _____ value.

We compare U_{obt} to _____. U_{obt} is not significant if it is _____

than U_{crit}.

The nonparametric version of the t-test for two independent samples

when an n is greater than 20 is the _____ _____ test. Here we

compute ΣR and ΣR_{exp} for _____ sample. In the _____-tailed

test, we predict ΣR will not equal ΣR_{exp}. In the one-tailed test, we predict

either ΣR will be only greater than or only less than _____. We

compute the statistic _____, and compare it to _____. We have a

significant z_{obt} if it is _____ than z_{crit}. If the relationship is

_____, we describe it by computing _____.

The nonparametric version of the t-test for two related samples is the

_____ _____ test. First, we determine the difference between

each pair of raw scores, and then we _____ the nonzero difference

scores. We then compute one ΣR for the ranks of the _____ difference

scores and one ΣR for the ranks of the _____ difference scores. In the

two-tailed test, the Wilcoxon T_{obt} is equal to the _____ ΣR. In the

one-tailed test, the ΣR we predict will be the _____ is the value of

T_{obt}. Then we compare T_{obt} to _____. T_{obt} is not significant if it is

_____ than T_{crit}.

Mann-Whitney U

each

smaller

smaller

U_{crit}; larger

rank sums

one; two

ΣR_{exp}

z_{obt}; z_{crit}

larger

significant; η^2

Wilcoxon T

rank

positive

negative

smaller

smaller

T_{crit}

larger

The nonparametric version of the one-way between-subjects ANOVA is

Kruskal-Walls H

the _____ _____ _____test. Here, we compute the

ΣR; sum

_____ in every condition. Then we compute the _____

of squares; H_{obt}

_____ _____. Finally, we compute the statistic _____. We

χ^2

compare H_{obt} to a critical value of _____. H_{obt} is significant if it is

larger

_____ than χ^2_{crit}. Post hoc comparisons are performed using the

rank sums

_____ _____ test. We describe the effect size by computing

η^2

_____.

The nonparametric version of the one-way within-subjects ANOVA is

Friedman χ^2; each

the _____ _____ test. First, we rank the scores of _____

condition

participant, and then we compute ΣR for each _____. We then

sum of squares

compute the _____ _____ _____. Finally, we compute the

χ^2_{obt}; χ^2_{crit}

statistic _____, which we compare to _____. χ^2_{obt} is significant

larger

if it is _____ than χ^2_{crit}. When χ^2_{obt} is significant, Nemenyi's

Tukey's HSD

procedure is analogous to _____ _____ procedure. We compute

critical

the "_____ difference." Then, any conditions in which the

mean ranks; more

_____ _____ differ by _____ than the critical difference

are significantly different. We describe the effect size by computing

η^2

_____.

NOW DO YOU KNOW?

f_{o} f_{e} χ^2_{obt} χ^2_{crit} Φ Φ^2 C C^2 ΣR ΣR_{exp}

nonparametric statistics

chi square procedure

one-way chi square

observed frequency

goodness-of-fit test

expected frequency

χ^2-distribution

two-way chi square

test of independence

phi coefficient

contingency coefficient

Mann-Whitney U

rank sums test

Wilcoxon T test

Kruskal-Wallis H test

Friedman χ^2 test

Nemenyi's procedure

USING WHAT YOU KNOW

1. a. What do we determine when we perform nonparametric statistics?
   b. When are they used?

2. a. When is the one-way χ^2 test used?
   b. When is the two-way χ^2 test used?

3. a. What are the symbol for and meaning of observed frequency?
   b. What are the symbol for and meaning of expected frequency?

4. a. What does a significant one-way χ^2 indicate?
   b. What does a significant two-way χ^2 indicate?

5. a. What is the phi coefficient and when is it used?
   b. What does the squared phi coefficient indicate?

6. a. What is the contingency coefficient and when is it used?
   b. What does the squared contingency coefficient indicate?

7. Which nonparametric test for ranks corresponds to each of the following parametric tests?

   a. The related samples t-test
   b. Fisher's protected t-test
   c. The t-test for independent samples, $n \leq 20$
   d. The one-way between subjects ANOVA
   e. The t-test for independent samples, $n > 20$
   f. Tukey's HSD
   g. The one-way within-subjects ANOVA

8. In which tests listed in problem 7 must the obtained value be equal to or smaller than the critical value in order for the results to be significant?

9.   Assume that each of the following studies cannot be analyzed using a parametric procedure.
      For each of the following studies, indicate the appropriate nonparametric procedure:

      a.   One group of 30 mommies has played classical music to their babies every day for 6
           months while another group of 30 mommies has not. They are tested to determine if there
           is a significant difference in the motor coordination skills of these two groups.
      b.   College freshmen with high test anxiety are randomly assigned to three groups. One group
           receives free individualized counseling, one group participates in a class to teach them to
           reduce their anxiety, and the third group receives no treatment. They are tested to determine
           if there is a significant difference in the test anxiety levels of these three groups.
      c.   Elementary school children with Attention Deficit Disorder are tested for their ability to
           read a 5-page age-appropriate document. Each child is then assigned to a reading tutor.
           After 3 weeks of working with the tutor, each child's reading ability is tested again.
      d.   A survey of local residents has been conducted to determine the level of support for a new
           shopping plaza. Those surveyed were allowed to respond in one of five categories—
           strongly support, support, no opinion, do not support, strongly do not support. The number
           of people in each category was recorded.
      e.   A Kruskal-Wallis H Test has indicated there is a significant relationship between the level
           of a cholesterol-lowering drug taken and the number of headaches reported. The
           researchers need to determine which pair(s) out of the 5 treatment levels used is(are)
           significantly different.

10.   Which parametric tests correspond to the following nonparametric tests?

      a.   The Mann-Whitney U test
      b.   The rank sums test
      c.   The Wilcoxon T test
      d.   The Kruskal-Wallis H test
      e.   The Friedman χ^2 test
      f.   Nemenyi's procedure

11.   A newspaper article claims that there are many more newborn females than males, although
      you had assumed that there was a 50-50 chance of being born male or female. Through the
      local hospital, you determine that 628 baby boys and 718 baby girls were born over the past
      two-month period.

      a.   What are H_0 and H_a?
      b.   Compute the appropriate statistic.
      c.   Determine whether the results are significant at $\alpha = 0.05$.
      d.   Report your results in the correct format and interpret them.

12. A researcher collected the following handedness data from 60 students. Determine whether gender and handedness are unrelated variables.

	Left-handed	Ambidextrous	Right-handed
Men	29	3	8
Women	1	9	10

   a. What are the null and alternative hypotheses?
   b. Compute the appropriate statistic.
   c. Determine whether the results are significant at $\alpha = 0.05$.
   d. Describe the strength of this relationship. How useful a relationship is it?
   e. Report and interpret the results.

13. a. Use the Mann-Whitney U test to perform a two-tailed analysis of the interval data listed below.

Sample A	Sample B
11	30
15	9
6	18
24	27
23	26
8	20

   b. What conclusions can be drawn from these results?

14. a. Perform a two-tailed Wilcoxon test using the following ratio scores (subtracting A – B):

Participant	Condition A	Condition B
1	25	38
2	23	21
3	19	36
4	7	12
5	21	21
6	9	28
7	11	33
8	18	17
9	10	29

   b. What conclusions can be drawn from these results?

15. In a recent report, Charlene's company claimed that they hire as many women as men engineers. Using the company's hiring information for the past year, Charlene (who is the Human Resources Manager) decides to test this claim.

	Men	Women
Number of Engineers Hired	23	17

   a. What test should Charlene use?
   b. What are her H_0 and H_a?
   c. Conduct the appropriate test. Use $\alpha = 0.05$
   d. What should Charlene conclude about her company's claim?

16. Michael wants to know if support for a local referendum is related to political party affiliation. He conducts a survey of 200 local residents and asks them their political party affiliation and whether they intend to vote for or against the referendum. The number of individuals in each cell is reported below.

	For	Against
Republican	16	54
Democrat	72	28
Other	27	3

   a. What test should Michael use?
   b. What are H_0 and H_a?
   c. Conduct the appropriate test. Use $\alpha = 0.05$.
   d. What should Michael conclude?

17. An experiment was conducted to determine whether it is easier to recall 3-letter or 5-letter nonsense syllables. Each participant learned both a 3-letter and a 5-letter nonsense-syllable list, after which the number of errors in recall was determined. After performing the F_{max} test, the error scores could not be assumed to have homogeneity of variance.

   a. Under these circumstances, which statistical test would be appropriate for analyzing these data?
   b. If the data were homogeneous, what would be the most powerful test?

THE TEST

1. The data that are required for χ^2 tests are

   a. frequencies of participants in categories.
   b. ranks of participants in two categories.
   c. interval data that have been ranked.
   d. mean rankings in two or more categories.

2. In a two-way χ^2, the expected frequencies represent the ideal distribution of frequencies that would occur if the variables were

    a. perfectly dependent.
    b. completely independent.
    c. measured as interval or ratio data.
    d. measured as ordinal or ranked data.

3. In researching the effect of working in a cubicle as opposed to a private office on the productivity of middle managers in a large corporation, you have collected data on 80 individuals (40 cubicle users and 40 private offices). After conducting an F_{max} test, you realize that you cannot assume homogeneity of variance. What test should you use to analyze your results?

    a. A Wilcoxon T test
    b. A rank sums test
    c. A Mann-Whitney U test
    d. An independent samples t-test

4. You have 20 students rank the talent of the 5 starters on the basketball team. What test can you use to determine whether these players differ in talent?

    a. A Mann-Whitney U test
    b. A rank sums test
    c. A Friedman χ^2 test
    d. A Wilcoxon T test

5. Which of the following nonparametric tests requires that the obtained value be smaller than the critical value in order to reject the null hypothesis?

    a. The rank sums test
    b. The Mann-Whitney U test
    c. The Friedman χ^2 test
    d. The 2 x 2 χ^2

ANSWERS TO USING WHAT YOU KNOW

1. a. Whether sample data are likely to represent the predicted relationship in the population.
    b. When the data do not meet the assumptions of a parametric procedure.

2. a. When the data reflect the frequency with which participants fall into the categories of one independent variable.
    b. When the data reflect the frequency with which participants fall into each cell formed by the categories from two independent variables.

3. a. Observed frequency is symbolized as f_o, the number of participants who fall into a category or cell.
    b. Expected frequency is symbolized as f_e, the expected number of participants who fall into a category or cell if the data perfectly represent the distribution described by H_0.

4. a. It indicates that the sample frequencies are unlikely to represent the distribution described by H_0 of frequencies in the population.
    b. It indicates that category membership on one variable depends on, or is correlated with, category membership on the other variable.

5. a. It is a correlation coefficient used to describe the strength of the relationship in a significant two-way χ^2 that involves a 2 x 2 design.
    b. Phi squared is the proportion of variance accounted for by the relationship between the two variables.

6. a. It is a correlation coefficient used to describe the strength of the relationship in a significant two-way χ^2 that does not involve a 2 x 2 design.
    b. The squared contingency coefficient is the proportion of variance accounted for by the relationship between the two variables.

7. a. The Wilcoxon T
    b. The rank sums test
    c. The Mann-Whitney U
    d. The Kruskal-Wallis H
    e. The rank sums test
    f. Nemenyi's procedure
    g. The Friedman χ^2

8. The Mann-Whitney U and the Wilcoxon T.

9. a. The rank sums test for two independent samples with either n greater than 20.
    b. The Kruskal-Wallis H test for three or more independent samples.
    c. The Wilcoxon T test for two related samples.
    d. The one-way chi square test.
    e. The rank sums test as a post hoc comparison to the Kruskal-Wallis H test.

10. a. The t-test for independent samples.
    b. The t-test for independent samples and Fisher's protected t-test.
    c. The t-test for related samples.
    d. The one-way, between-subjects ANOVA.
    e. The one-way, within-subjects ANOVA.
    f. Tukey's HSD test.

11. a. H_0: the samples represent equal frequencies in the population; H_a: the samples represent unequal frequencies in the population.
    b. $f_e = 1{,}346/2 = 673$, $\chi^2_{obt} = (628 - 673)^2/673 + (718 - 673)^2/673 = 6.02$.
    c. For $df = 1$, $\chi^2_{crit} = 3.84$, and so results are significant.
    d. $\chi^2(1) = 6.02, p < 0.05$. There is evidence that the frequency of males and females born in the population is not equal. Rather, based on our sample, we expect that 628/1,346, or 47%, are male, and 718/1,346, or 53%, are female.

12. a. H_0 : the variables are independent; H_a : the variables are dependent.
     b. $\chi^2_{obt} = 81/20 + 25/8 + 16/12 + 81/10 + 25/4 + 16/6 = 25.53$.
     c.   For $df = 2$, $\chi^2_{crit} = 5.99$, so reject H_0.
     d.   On a scale of 0 to ± 1.0, the strength of this relationship is $C = \sqrt{25.53/85.53} = 0.55$. It is reasonably useful because $C^2 = 0.30$.
     e. $\chi^2 (2) = 25.53, p < 0.05$. The frequencies of gender and handedness are likely to be related or correlated in the population, and the relationship is relatively strong in the sample.

13. a. $U_1 = 36 + 21 - 49 = 8$; $U_2 = 36 + 21 - 29 = 28$, so $U_{obt} = 8$. $U_{crit} = 5$, so retain H_0.
     b.   There is no evidence that the two samples represent different populations of ranks or different populations of interval scores.

14. a.   Sum of positive ranks = 3, sum of negative ranks = 33, $T = 3$. For $N = 8$, $T_{crit} = 3$.
     b.   The ranks differ significantly, and so we can be confident that the samples of ratio scores represent different populations that would occur under the two conditions.

15. a.   She should use a one-way chi square test.
     b. H_0 : all frequencies in the population are equal.

          H_a : not all frequencies in the population are equal.

     c. $f_e = \dfrac{40}{2} = 20$

          $\chi^2_{obt} = \dfrac{(23-20)^2}{20} + \dfrac{(17-20)^2}{20} = 0.45 + 0.45 = 0.90$

          χ^2_{crit} for $df = 2 - 1$ is 3.84. Since χ^2_{obt} is not greater than χ^2_{crit}, we fail to reject the H_0.

     d.   Charlene should conclude that there is insufficient evidence to dispute her company's claim that they hire as many women as men engineers.

16. a.   He should use a two-way chi square test.
     b. H_0 : Category membership on the two variables in the population is independent.
          H_a : Category membership on the two variables in the population is dependent.
     c.

f_e	For	Against
Republican	$\dfrac{(70)(115)}{200} = 40.25$	$\dfrac{(70)(85)}{200} = 29.75$
Democrat	$\dfrac{(100)(115)}{200} = 57.50$	$\dfrac{(100)(85)}{200} = 42.50$
Other	$\dfrac{(30)(115)}{200} = 17.25$	$\dfrac{(30)(85)}{200} = 12.75$

$$\chi^2_{obt} = \frac{(16-40.25)^2}{40.25} + \frac{(54-29.75)^2}{29.75} + \frac{(72-57.50)^2}{57.50} + \frac{(28-42.50)^2}{42.50} + \frac{(27-17.25)^2}{17.25} +$$

$$\frac{(3-12.75)^2}{17.25} = 14.610 + 19.767 + 3.657 + 4.947 + 5.511 + 5.511 = 54.003$$

χ^2_{crit} for $(3-1)(2-1) = 2$ is 5.99. Since $\chi^2_{obt} > \chi^2_{crit}$, we reject H_0.

   d. Michael should conclude that support for the referendum is dependent on party affiliation.

17.   a. The Wilcoxon T.
      b. The related samples t-test.

ANSWERS TO THE TEST

   1. a   2. b   3. b   4. c   5. b

Getting Ready for the Final Exam

YOU SHOULD KNOW

1. The characteristics of the different measurement scales and the appropriate methods of graphing and describing central tendency for each.

2. What variance and standard deviation tell us about a sample or population and how z-scores are used to describe the relative location of a score on the standard normal curve.

3. What a significant correlation coefficient tells us and how r and r_s are tested and used.

4. What the linear regression line describes, how it is used to predict scores, and what is meant by the proportion of variance accounted for.

5. The logic of statistical hypothesis testing and how Type I errors, Type II errors, and power affect the decisions we make about relationships.

6. When to perform the z-test and the single-sample t-test and how to interpret significant results.

7. When to perform the t-test for independent samples and the t-test for related samples and how to interpret significant results.

8. When to perform the one-way between-subjects ANOVA and the within-subjects ANOVA, when to use post hoc comparisons, and how to interpret significant results.

9. When to perform the two-way between-subjects ANOVA and post hoc comparisons, and how to interpret significant main effects and interactions.

10. How to compute and interpret confidence intervals and measures of effect size.

11. When to use the one-way and the two-way chi square, how to interpret significant results, and how to describe the relationship using Φ and C.

12. When to use the Mann-Whitney U, the rank sums test, the Wilcoxon T, the Kruskal-Wallis H, the Friedman χ^2, and related post hoc comparisons and measures of effect size.

USING WHAT YOU KNOW

1. What is the difference between a statistic and a parameter?

2. a. For what purpose are descriptive statistics used?
    b. For what purpose are inferential statistics used?

3. a. What are the two types of inferential statistics?
    b. When is each used?
    c. Which type is generally preferred and why?

4. a. What is an independent variable?
    b. What is a dependent variable?
    c. What does it mean in terms of the relationship between two variables to say that the scores on the dependent variable change significantly as a function of the independent variable?

5. Why is random sampling so important in statistics?

6. a. What are simple frequency, relative frequency, and cumulative frequency?
    b. What does a percentile indicate?

7. List and define the four scales of measurement.

8. a. Describe a line graph and a bar graph.
    b. When is each used?

9. What is the difference between a positively skewed distribution and a negatively skewed distribution?

10. What two types of descriptive measures must we compute to describe any sample?

11. a. What do measures of central tendency indicate?
    b. Name and define the three measures of central tendency.
    c. When do we use each of these measures?

12. a. What do we mean by the concept of variability?
    b. What is the usual reference point for measuring variability?
    c. List the three most common measures of variability.

13. a. Distinguish among the symbols $S, \sigma,$ and s as they apply to the standard deviation and variance.
    b. What is the relationship between the standard deviation and the variance?
    c. State two reasons why we most often use the standard deviation to describe variability.

14. For what three reasons is it useful to transform raw scores into z-scores?

15. a. What two things do we learn from a linear correlation coefficient?
    b. Explain this statement: As the coefficient approaches ± 1.0, the strength of the relationship increases.
    c. Distinguish among the use of r and r_s.

16. Why is it important to avoid the restriction-of-range problem?

17. a. What is the purpose of a regression analysis?
    b. When is it appropriate to compute the regression equation?
    c. How are errors in prediction measured in regression analysis?
    d. What is homoscedasticity?

18. a. On what do we base the probability of an event?
    b. What does probability communicate about an event in a random sample?

19. What is sampling error?

20. Why is statistical hypothesis testing necessary?

21. a. What does H_0 describe?
    b. What does H_a describe?

22. Describe the general logic of statistical hypothesis testing in terms a nonstatistician would understand.

23. a. What does a sampling distribution indicate?
    b. What is the critical value?
    c. What is the region of rejection?
    d. What is alpha?

24. What does *significant* mean?

25. a. When do we use one-tailed tests and two-tailed tests?
    b. How does each type of test affect how a sampling distribution is set up?

26. a. Define a Type I error.
    b. Describe the pitfalls associated with Type I errors in terms of the conclusions drawn about the relationship between the independent and dependent variables.
    c. How can the probability of making a Type I error be reduced?

27. a. Define a Type II error.
    b. Describe the pitfalls associated with Type II errors in terms of the conclusions drawn about the relationship between the independent and dependent variables.
    c. How can the probability of making a Type II error be reduced?

28. a. When you claim that a result is significant, what is the error you may have made? What is the error you may have avoided?
    b. When you fail to reject H_0, what is the error you may have made? What is the error you may have avoided?

29. a. What is power?
    b. What is the general strategy for maximizing power?
    c. Why does this strategy increase power?

30.   a.   What two parametric tests are used to test hypotheses about one-sample experiments?
      b.   When is each test used?
      c.   If there are nonparametric versions of these tests, what are they?

31.   a.   What two parametric tests are used to test hypotheses about two sample means?
      b.   When is each used?
      c.   If there are nonparametric versions of these tests, what are they?

32.   a.   What parametric test is used to test hypotheses about three or more sample means from one independent variable?
      b.   When are the between-subjects and the within-subjects versions of this test used?
      c.   If there are nonparametric versions of these tests, what are they?

33.   a.   What are the components of the F-ratio?
      b.   What does a significant F-ratio indicate?

34.   a.   When do you perform the one-way ANOVA? The two-way ANOVA?
      b.   What additional information is obtained from the two-way ANOVA that cannot be obtained from separate one-way ANOVAs?
      c.   What does this significant effect indicate?
      d.   What are the differences among a between-subjects, a within-subjects, and a mixed-design ANOVA?

35.   a.   When there are more than two levels in a significant factor, what additional tests are required?
      b.   What are the two parametric versions of these tests and what determines which one we use?
      c.   If there are nonparametric versions of these tests, what are they and when are they used?

36.   What is homogeneity of variance?

37.   a.   In any statistical procedure, after obtaining a significant result, what should you do next?
      b.   List the three types of procedures that enable you to do this.

38.   a.   What is a confidence interval?
      b.   Why is a confidence interval better than point estimation?
      c.   List the three types of confidence intervals you have learned.

39.   a.   What is meant by the proportion of variance accounted for?
      b.   What is computed to measure this in correlational procedures?
      c.   What is computed to measure this in the two-sample t-test?
      d.   What is computed to measure this in ANOVA to describe the sample?
      e.   What is computed to measure this in χ^2 ?
      f.   What is computed to measure this in nonparametric ranked-score statistics?
      g.   In experiments, what is another name for the proportion of variance accounted for?

40.   a.   When is the chi square test used?
      b.   What is the difference between a one-way chi square and a two-way chi square?
      c.   What does Φ describe and when is it used?
      d.   What does C describe and when is it used?

41. a. Construct a frequency distribution table for the following data set. Include the simple frequency (*f*), the relative frequency (rel. *f*), and the cumulative frequency (*cf*).

8	10	9	15	11	13	12	15
9	8	12	8	14	13	8	

b. Find the mode, median, and mean ($\overline{X}$) of this data set.
c. Find the range and the estimated population standard deviation (*s*) of this data set.

42. Assume the data set in problem 41 represents a random sample. Conduct the appropriate test to determine whether this sample is representative of a population with $\mu = 9$. Use a two-tailed test with $\alpha = 0.05$.

43. A researcher randomly assigns 10 people to each of two groups. One group receives a treatment and the other group does not. Using the data given below, conduct the appropriate test to determine if there is a significant difference between the two group means. Use a two-tailed test with $\alpha = 0.05$.

Treatment	No Treatment
8	6
7	5
8	6
8	6
6	5
7	5
8	6
5	4
7	4
8	7

44. A researcher measures 10 individuals prior to and after receiving treatment. Using the data given below, conduct the appropriate test to determine if there is a significant difference between the Before Treatment and After Treatment.

Before Treatment	After Treatment
8	6
7	5
8	6
8	6
6	5
7	5
8	6
5	4
7	4
8	7

45.   A study has been conducted to determine the effectiveness of three levels of treatment (on three groups of people). The data are given below.

Level 1	Level 2	Level 3
2	4	3
2	4	2
4	4	2
3	3	3
2	2	3
4	4	2
2	5	3

a.   Conduct the appropriate test to determine if there is a significant difference among the treatment means.

b.   Based on your findings in part a, what else should you do?

46.   Use the data and results from problem 45.

a.   If appropriate, compute the post hoc comparisons.

b.   If appropriate, compute the effect size.

47.   Suppose you have collected information on two continuous variables. Your data are given below.

X	Y
1	8
2	5
3	6
4	7
5	6
6	5
7	4
8	3
9	1
10	3

a.   Calculate the correct procedure to determine the strength of the relationship between these two variables.

b.   Conduct an inferential test to determine whether or not this is a significant relationship. Use a two-tailed test and $\alpha = 0.05$.

48. A team of researchers has conducted a study to determine whether three levels of Drug D and two levels of Vitamin Supplement M affect ability to mentally compute simple math problems. There are eight different participants in each cell. The data are given below.

| | Drug D | | | | | |
Vitamin Supplement M	Level 1		Level 2		Level 3	
Level 1	2	1	2	1	2	3
	0	1	1	2	3	2
	2	2	2	2	3	3
	1	3	2	1	1	3
Level 2	3	2	2	3	0	1
	0	3	3	2	1	1
	1	3	3	1	1	0
	3	1	1	2	0	0

a. What is (are) the independent variable(s)?
    What is (are) the dependent variables(s)?
b. Conduct the appropriate test to determine if there is a significant difference among the treatment means. Use $\alpha = 0.05$.
c. Based on your results in part b, what else should you do?

49. A professor of nutrition and her students have obtained some data on cholesterol levels. They want to determine if there is a significant ($p < 0.05$) difference between older men versus older women (older than age 65) in whether their HDL (good cholesterol) is above the recommended minimum level. The data for number of people in each cell are presented below.

	Below Minimum	Above Minimum	
Men	40	60	100
Women	20	80	100
	60	140	

a. What is χ^2_{obt}?
b. What is the critical value found in the table?
c. Is χ^2_{obt} significant at $p < 0.05$?
d. What is Φ?
e. How should the professor and her students interpret their findings?

50.   The following five scenarios all involve ranks (ranked data). Which nonparametric test is appropriate for each scenario?

    a.   There were 4 independent samples of runners (age brackets A, B, C, and D). Their running times were ranked. What nonparametric test should be used?
    b.   There were 2 independent samples of Science Fair projects (40 Life-Science projects and 40 Physical-Science projects). Their scores from the judging were ranked. What nonparametric test should be used?
    c.   There were 5 repeated measures samples of logic problems (Problems 1, 2, 3, 4, 5), which each of the 50 participants tried to solve. Their scores (quality/quantity points) on the logic problems were ranked. What nonparametric test should be used?
    d.   There were 2 related samples of parent–child opinions (e.g., mother–son) in which each expressed opinions about social problems in society. Each person's score on the social problems test was ranked by a panel of experts. What nonparametric test should be used?
    e.   There were 2 independent samples of high-school students (16 members of the Honor Society and 16 members of the Drama Club). Their hours of participation in school extra-curricular activities were ranked. What nonparametric test should be used?

ANSWERS TO USING WHAT YOU KNOW

1.   A statistic describes a characteristic of a sample, and a parameter describes a characteristic of a population.

2.   a.   To organize, summarize, and communicate information about data.
      b.   To test hypotheses about the relationship in the population represented by the sample data.

3.   a.   Parametric and nonparametric.
      b.   Parametric statistics are used when the scores are measured using ratio or interval scales and the populations are normally distributed and have homogeneous variance. Nonparametric statistics are used when nominal or ordinal scales are used, or when the populations of interval or ratio data are skewed or have heterogeneous variance.
      c.   Parametric, because they are more powerful.

4.   a.   A variable that is manipulated by the experimenter.
      b.   A variable that is measured by the experimenter.
      c.   In the experiment, the scores on the dependent variable change in a certain way as the conditions of the independent variable change, and we are confident that this relationship would be found in the population.

5.   Because all statistical procedures are based on the assumption that the sample has been randomly selected from the population.

6.   a.   Simple frequency is the number of times a score occurs. Relative frequency is the proportion of the time that a score occurs out of all scores. Cumulative frequency is the number of scores at or below a particular score.
      b.   The percentage of all scores at or below a score.

7.   Nominal: Each score does not actually indicate an amount; rather, it is used simply for identification. Ordinal: Rank-ordered scores indicate a relative amount, with no zero and no consistent unit of measurement. Interval: Scores measure a quantity using a consistent unit of measurement, but zero is not truly a zero amount, and there can be negative numbers. Ratio: Scores measure a quantity using a consistent unit of measurement, a zero indicates a zero amount, and there cannot be negative numbers.

8.   a.   In a line graph, adjacent data points are connected with straight lines; in a bar graph, each data point is identified by a vertical bar, and adjacent bars do not touch each other.
      b.   Line graphs are used when the independent variable (or X variable) is an interval or ratio variable; bar graphs are used when it is a nominal or ordinal variable.

9.   A positively skewed distribution is nonsymmetrical, with only the extreme high scores having a relatively low frequency. In a negatively skewed distribution, only the extreme low scores have a relatively low frequency.

10.   We must compute a measure of central tendency and a measure of variability.

11.   a.   They indicate the location of a distribution on the variable and the score around which the distribution tends to be centered.
      b.   The mean, the average score in a distribution; the mode, the most frequently occurring score; and the median, the score at the 50th percentile.
      c.   The mean is used when interval or ratio data are approximately normally or symmetrically distributed; the mode is used with nominal data; and the median is used with ordinal data, or when an interval/ratio distribution is very skewed.

12.   a.   The differences between the scores in a distribution.
      b.   The difference between each score and the mean.
      c.   The range, the variance, and the standard deviation.

13.   a. S describes the sample, s is an estimate of the population, and σ is the true population parameter.
      b.   The standard deviation is the square root of the variance.
      c.   The standard deviation is measured in the same units as the scores (variance is measured in squared units), and the standard deviation relates directly to the area under the standard normal curve.

14.   To make scores from different variables comparable, to enable use of the standard normal curve model, and to define psychological attributes.

15.   a.   The strength and direction of the relationship between two variables.
      b.   As the correlation coefficient approaches ±1.0, there increasingly tends to be one value of Y consistently associated with one and only one value of X.
      c. r is used when both variables are interval or ratio variables and r_s is used when both variables are ordinal variables.

16.   With restricted range, the correlation coefficient is artificially low, resulting in an underestimate of the strength of the relationship between the variables.

17. a. To make predictions about scores on one variable using the scores on a correlated variable.
    b. When the obtained correlation coefficient is statistically significant.
    c. As the differences between each Y' and the corresponding Y scores, summarized as the standard error of the estimate, $S_{Y'}$.
    d. The assumption that the spread in Y scores around each corresponding Y' is equal.

18. a. On the relative frequency of the event in the population.
    b. The event's expected relative frequency in samples and our confidence that the event will or will not occur.

19. Any difference between a sample statistic and the population parameter it represents that occurs because of chance when randomly selecting the sample.

20. To decide whether the sample data accurately represent the predicted relationship in the population or, because of sampling error, poorly represent the absence of the relationship.

21. a. The values of the population parameters represented by the sample statistics if the predicted relationship does not exist.
    b. The values of the population parameters represented by the sample statistics if the predicted relationship does exist.

22. Using a model of how sample data are distributed, we determine the likelihood of obtaining sample data such as ours when only chance is operating and the data do not represent the predicted relationship in nature. If data such as ours are too unlikely to occur in such a situation, we reject the chance explanation and conclude that our data occurred because they represent the predicted relationship.

23. a. The frequencies of the values of a sample statistic that occur by chance when the sample represents the population described by H_0.
    b. The value of the inferential statistic that marks the beginning of the region of rejection.
    c. The portion of the sampling distribution containing sample statistics that are defined as too unlikely to accept as representative of the population parameters described by H_0.
    d. The criterion probability that defines "too unlikely," the size of the region of rejection, and the theoretical probability of a Type I error.

24. It means that sample data such as ours are too unlikely to occur to accept that the data represent the populations described by H_0. Instead, the data are likely to represent populations described by H_a, which are the populations that occur when the predicted relationship exists in nature.

25. a. We use one-tailed tests when we predict the direction of the relationship represented by our data. We use two-tailed tests when we do not predict the direction of the relationship.
    b. In a one-tailed test, the entire region of rejection is placed into one tail of the sampling distribution, and we use only the positive or negative critical value. In a two-tailed test, one-half of the region of rejection is placed into each tail, and we use both the positive and negative critical values.

26. a. Rejecting the null hypothesis when it is really true.
    b. You conclude that a relationship exists between the variables in nature, when in reality one does not.
    c. By reducing the alpha level.

27.   a.   Failing to reject the null hypothesis when it is really false.
      b.   You fail to find evidence for the relationship, although the relationship exists in nature.
      c.   By increasing a study's power.

28.   a.   Type I; Type II.
      b.   Type II; Type I.

29.   a.   The probability of rejecting the null hypothesis when it is really false.
      b.   Use sufficient N and design studies to maximize between-group differences and minimize within-group differences.
      c.   The obtained result is more likely to be significant.

30.   a.   The z-test and the single-sample t-test.
      b.   The z-test is used when the population standard deviation or variance is known; the t-test is used when the population standard deviation or variance is estimated from the sample.
      c.   There are none.

31.   a.   The t-test for independent samples and the t-test for related samples.
      b.   For independent samples, the scores in one sample are not influenced by the scores in the other sample. For related samples, either participants in one sample are paired or matched with those in the other sample, or the same participants are tested under both conditions of the experiment.
      c.   For independent samples, the Mann-Whitney U when $n \leq 20$ and the rank sums test when $n > 20$. For related samples, the Wilcoxon T.

32.   a.   The ANOVA.
      b.   The between-subjects version is used when independent samples serve in each condition, and the within-subjects version is used when related samples are tested.
      c.   The Kruskal-Wallis H for between-subjects and the Friedman χ^2 for within-subjects.

33.   a.   The MS_{bn} and the MS_{wn}.
      b.   It indicates that the differences between the means are unlikely to reflect mere random variability in scores (error variance), but rather that they represent differences between populations (treatment variance); therefore, at least two means represent different values of μ.

34.   a.   The one-way ANOVA is used when the experiment involves one independent variable. The two-way ANOVA is used with two independent variables.
      b.   Information about the interaction between the variables.
      c.   It indicates that the levels of one independent variable influence the relationship between the other independent variable and the dependent scores.
      d.   In a between-subjects design, all cells involve independent samples; in a within-subjects design, all cells involve related samples; and in a mixed design, one factor is a between-subjects factor and the other is a within-subjects factor.

35. a. Post hoc comparisons.
    b. Fisher's protected t-test, used when ns are unequal, and Tukey's HSD, used when all ns are equal.
    c. The nonparametric version of Fisher's protected t-test is the rank sums test, used with the Kruskal-Wallis H. The nonparametric version of Tukey's HSD test is Nemenyi's procedure, used with Friedman's χ^2 test.

36. The assumption that the variances of the populations represented by the samples are equal.

37. a. Describe the relationship you have demonstrated.
    b. Graphing the results, computing the effect size, and computing confidence intervals.

38. a. An interval containing a range of values of a population parameter, one of which the sample statistic is likely to represent.
    b. Confidence intervals take into account that the sample may reflect sampling error; point estimation does not.
    c. The confidence interval for a single μ, for the difference between two μs, and for the μ of difference scores.

39. a. The proportion of the total variability in Y scores that can be accounted for or predicted by using the relationship with X.
    b. The squared correlation coefficient is computed.
    c. r_{pb}^2 is computed.
    d. η^2 is computed.
    e. Φ^2 or C^2 is computed.
    f. η^2 is computed.
    g. The effect size.

40. a. When the data reflect the frequency with which participants fall into the categories of one or more variables.
    b. The one-way tests goodness of fit on one variable; that is, whether the samples represent the distribution of frequencies described by H_0. The two-way tests for independence of two variables; that is, whether the frequency of category membership on one variable is independent or dependent on the frequency of category membership on the other variable.
    c. The strength of the relationship in a significant χ^2, used in a 2 x 2 design.
    d. The strength of the relationship in a significant χ^2, used in a two-way design that is not a 2 x 2.

41. a.

Score	f	rel. f	cf
15	2	0.13	15
14	1	0.07	13
13	2	0.13	12
12	2	0.13	10
11	1	0.07	7
10	1	0.07	7
9	2	0.13	6
8	4	0.27	4

b. Mode $= 8$, Median $= 11$, $\overline{X} = \dfrac{165}{15} = 11$

c. Range $= 7$

$$s = \sqrt{\dfrac{1{,}911 - \dfrac{(165)^2}{15}}{14}} = 2.62$$

42. $s_{\overline{X}} = \dfrac{2.62}{\sqrt{15}} = 0.677$ $t_{obt} = \dfrac{11-9}{0.677} = 2.95$ $t(14) = 2.92, p < 0.05$. Therefore, there is sufficient

evidence to conclude that this sample does not represent a population with $\mu = 9$.

43. $\overline{X}_1 = 7.200$ $s_1^2 = 1.067$

$\overline{X}_2 = 5.400$ $s_2^2 = 0.933$

$$s_{pool}^2 = \dfrac{(9)\,1.067 + (9)\,0.993}{9+9} = \dfrac{18}{18} = 1$$

$$s_{\overline{X}_1 - \overline{X}_2} = \sqrt{1\left(\dfrac{1}{10} + \dfrac{1}{10}\right)} = 0.447$$

$$t_{obt} = \dfrac{7.20 - 5.40}{0.4471} = 4.03$$

$t(17) = 4.03, p < 0.05$. There is a significant difference between the two means.

44. $\overline{D}=\dfrac{18}{10}=1.80$ $s_D^2=\dfrac{36-\dfrac{18^2}{10}}{9}=0.40$

$s_{\overline{D}}=\sqrt{\dfrac{0.40}{10}}=0.20$

$t_{obt}=\dfrac{1.80}{0.20}=9.00$

$t(9)=9.00, p<0.05$. There is a significant difference between the Before Treatment and the After Treatment means.

45.   a.

Source	Sum of Squares	df	Mean Square	F
Between Groups	5.429	2	2.714	3.89
Within Groups	12.571	18	0.698	
Total	18.000	20		

The one-way between-subjects ANOVA is significant at $\alpha=0.05$.

   b.   Because the ANOVA is significant, you should do a post hoc test (Tukey *HSD*) to determine where the differences occur. You also should determine the effect size.

46.   a. $HSD=3.58\left(\sqrt{\dfrac{0.698}{7}}\right)=3.58(\sqrt{0.0997})=3.58(0.316)=1.130$

The means were $\overline{X}_1=2.714$
$\overline{X}_2=3.714$
$\overline{X}_3=2.571$

Therefore, Level 1 and Level 2 do not differ significantly.
Level 1 and Level 3 do not differ significantly.
Level 2 and Level 3 differ significantly ($p<0.05$).

   b.   eta squared

$\eta^2=\dfrac{5.429}{18.000}=0.302$

47.   a. $r=\dfrac{10(215)-(55)(48)}{\sqrt{[10(385)-55^2][10(270)-48^2}}=\dfrac{-490}{\sqrt{(825)(396)}}=\dfrac{-490}{571.58}=-0.857$

   b. $r_{crit}=-0.632$ where $df=8$. There is a significant correlation between the two variables.

48.   a.   The two independent variables are Levels of Drug D and Levels of Vitamin Supplement M. The dependent variable is the ability to mentally compute simple math problems.

      b.

Source	Sum of Squares	df	Mean Square	F
Between Groups				
Levels of Drug D	1.167	2	0.584	0.85
Levels of Vitamin M	1.334	1	1.334	1.95
Drug D x Vitamin M	16.666	2	8.333	12.17
Within Groups	28.750	42	0.685	
Total	47.917			

The main effect for Levels of Drug D was not significant.
The main effect for Levels of Vitamin M was not significant.
The interaction of Levels of Drug D by Levels of Vitamin M was significant.

      c.   You should conduct a Tukey's *HSD* post hoc test, then calculate η^2 and a confidence interval for the significant interaction.

49.   a. $\chi^2_{obt} = 9.524$

      b. $\chi^2_{crit} = 3.84$ where $df = 1$

      c.   Yes

      d. $\Phi = 0.218$

      e.   There is a significant difference ($p < 0.05$) in which more of the older women were above the minimum than were the older men. The phi coefficient (which is analogous to a correlation) was 0.218, showing a moderate relationship.

50.   a.   The Kruskal-Wallis *H* test
      b.   The rank sums test
      c.   The Friedman χ^2 test
      d.   The Wilcoxon *T* test
      e.   The Mann-Whitney *U* test